IMAGES OF ENGLAND

REFLECTIONS OF BOGNOR REGIS

IMAGES OF ENGLAND

REFLECTIONS OF BOGNOR REGIS

SYLVIA ENDACOTT and SHIRLEY LEWIS

Dedicated to local historians of all ages.

Frontispiece: Bognor's place in the sun.

First published in 2007 by Tempus Publishing

Reprinted in 2012 by
The History Press
The Mill, Brimscombe Port,
Stroud, Gloucestershire, GL5 2QG
www.thehistorypress.co.uk

© Sylvia Endacott and Shirley Lewis, 2012

The right of Sylvia Endacott and Shirley Lewis to be identified as the Authors of this work has been asserted in accordance with the Copyrights, Designs and Patents Act 1988.

All rights reserved. No part of this book may be reprinted or reproduced or utilised in any form or by any electronic, mechanical or other means, now known or hereafter invented, including photocopying and recording, or in any information storage or retrieval system, without the permission in writing from the Publishers.

British Library Cataloguing in Publication Data.
A catalogue record for this book is available from the British Library.

ISBN 978 0 7524 4299 0

Typesetting and origination by
Tempus Publishing Limited.
Printed in Great Britain.

Contents

	Acknowledgements	6
	Introduction	7
one	The Founder	9
two	Personalities	15
three	Learning	23
four	Living	35
five	Shopping	47
six	Recreation	67
seven	Travel	87
eight	Holiday Accommodation	95
nine	The Villages	107

Acknowledgements

This book has been made possible by the generosity of many people who have lent family photographs, postcards, prints, sketches etc, to allow us to provide these images, enabling the reader to understand the progress that has been made since the arrival of Sir Richard Hotham.

We have endeavoured to trace the ownership of all photographs but if we have inadvertently missed one, we apologise. Many of the images used are from the joint collection of Sylvia Endacott and Shirley Lewis who have been inveterate collectors since their arrival in the town.

Special thanks are due to: Bognor Regis Local History Society, University of Chichester, Bognor Campus and Felpham and Middleton Local History Group.

The following individuals have agreed to their illustrations being included: David Bone, Carol Bradley, Reg Came, Janet Carter, Peter Christmas, Jim Clevett, Barbara Densley, Derek Frampton, Christine and Pat Fossey, Kay Fall, Peter Green, Tom Gillespie, Shirley Hardy, June Hayter, Don Hansford, Matthew Hansford, Trevor Jennings, Sue Kidd, Jane Lawrence, Denise Lickorish, Enso Macari, Norman Reynolds, Amanda Russell, Ken Scutt, Ken Sutton and Gill Woodruff.

Thanks also to the following for their help, assistance, encouragement and support: Moe Bone, Bob & Mil Chimley, Alex Clouter, Andrew Foster, Sheila Gould, Ron Iden, Brian Lewis, Simon Roberts, Trica Smith.

And finally to Barbara Bone, who died recently, for all her support to us over the years. Her expertise will be sadly missed.

Introduction

Over the centuries, people from all walks of life have been drawn to Bognor Regis for their own reasons. Two very notable individuals have, in their own ways, put their own personal stamp on this popular Sussex resort. First and foremost of these was Sir Richard Hotham. Instrumental in the development of some really splendid Regency buildings, he was responsible for truly putting Bognor (as it was then called) on the eighteenth-century Sussex map as a desirable coastal resort. Sir Richard Hotham is considered to be the town's founder and his legacy can still be seen on the sea front and inland.

King George V bestowed the additional name of 'Regis' to the town where he convalesced for around thirteen weeks in 1929. This was in recognition of the ambience, facilities and general well-being he enjoyed in and around the area now called Bognor Regis.

Of course there are many others who have contributed to the town's growth to make Bognor Regis what it is right now. They added a new dimension in home lifestyles, transportation and entertainment variety to those who migrated away from the big cities either to live somewhere restful and more permanent or just to enjoy a different sort of holiday.

We all know of Billy Butlin and the impact he made to bring bucket loads of holiday makers to Bognor Regis. If he could just see now the all-new Shoreline Hotel and Skyline built to cutting-edge designs. Do you know Arthur Davies who operated the first bus service in the town which evolved to the more familiar Southdown Bus Company? What about Joscelyn Hansford and Samuel Reynolds who were involved 'in trade' but also various organisations in the town? How about William Tate, known as the 'maker of Bognor Regis' whose business was to build the Princess Mary Memorial Home, the Arcade, the Kursaal and many other developments? Finally, not to be forgotten is Gerard Young, the man who popularised local history for so many people including ourselves.

We were drawn to Bognor Regis just like many others. We arrived here in the 1970s to work at Butlin's Holiday Camp, like so many people in the town. Although our origins come from elsewhere, we certainly have the Bognor blood inside. We are passionate about local history and became actively involved in the Bognor Regis Local History Society in 1979.

This book will give you an incredible journey back in time to read about the start and growth of Bognor Regis and its surrounding villages to what it is today – a thriving yet relaxing resort enjoyed by its local population and the many visitors that come for the entertainment, accommodation and many interests. We have captured areas of the town up to the 1970s as people enjoy history 'within living memory'.

This is our first joint publication. Sylvia has provided historical talks in the area since 1981 and written weekly articles in the *Bognor Regis Observer* since 1999. Shirley has been involved in local history research and produced a wide range of excellent exhibitions and displays at various events. We were for three years from 2003 to 2005, the organisers of the 'Festival of Local History' which encouraged an awareness and interest in local history.

Both of us have immensely enjoyed compiling the many photographs and articles that make up this book. We hope you will take equal pleasure in reading this book at leisure, looking at the many faces of the people and the buildings over the centuries that have made Bognor Regis what it is today.

Sylvia Endacott and Shirley Lewis

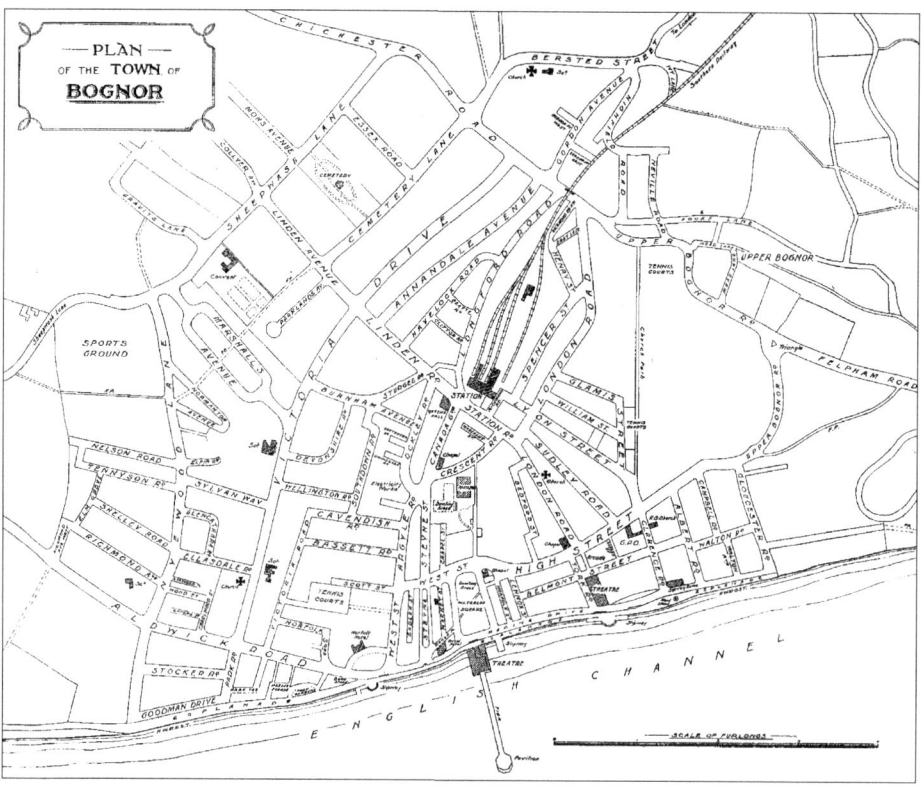

one

The Founder

Most seaside resorts are unaware of their origins. However, for Bognor Regis there is a definitive birthday and founder. Sir Richard Hotham arrived in the area from Merton, Surrey in 1787.

This is the only known painting of Sir Richard Hotham, which currently hangs in the Town Hall. This picture allegedly shows him leaning on his 'plan for Bognor'.

Following his career as a ship's husband with the East India Company and a period as a Member of Parliament for Southwark, London, he decided to look for a retirement area. In failing health, he alighted on a small fishing village with potential and thus commenced building his dream.

This inscription written by the Revd Thomas Durnford is in the South Bersted Parish Register and records the laying of the foundation stone of the public bathing place on 18 January 1787, thus providing the town with a unique record of its beginnings.

This is an early engraving of the house which is today used as the logo for the Hotham Park Heritage Trust. The Trust's aim is to retain the park area, once the gardens of Sir Richard Hotham, for future generations.

This view is only seen by those who work on the clock. The setting dial of the clock movement shows that it was made by John Thwaites of Clerkenwell, London in 1794 for Sir Richard Hotham, Knight. It cost £142 6s 10d. It was hand wound until 1994. The climb to the top of the tower is by ladders with sixty-one rungs in total.

Above: Mordington was built by Sir Richard Hotham *c.*1787 and was initially two private residences. Today it is a Grade II Listed Building. It was originally one of a crescent of three houses known as Hothamton Crescent, the other two being The Dome and St Michael's.

Left: This 2006 picture shows the coat of arms above the front of The Dome, still marking the influence of Sir Richard Hotham.

Sir Richard eventually moved further west in the town and built Hothamton Place during the 1790s which consisted of seven houses. By 1877 the terrace was purchased by the Merchant Taylors' to be used as a women's convalescent home. In 1921 the town council turned the building into flats, which proved not to be financially viable and they were finally demolished in 1935/6 to create a forecourt to the Pavilion entertainment complex.

This sketch of The Dome was created in 1946 by J.O. Langstone when he was a first year student at the newly formed teacher training college. It became known as the West Sussex Institute for Higher Education and today forms the Bognor campus of the University of Chichester.

Committee members of the Bognor Regis Local History Society, 1985. Pictured are: Sylvia Endacott, John Hawkins and pupils from the South Bersted Junior School, with the Revd Pruen behind the gravestone. This annual wreath-laying ceremony on 18 January at Sir Richard Hotham's grave always includes pupils from local schools. The materials for the wreath are traditionally collected from Hotham Park by members of the Local History Society.

This postcard, which was not produced until around 1890, depicts a view of 1815 showing the earliest buildings created by Sir Richard Hotham.

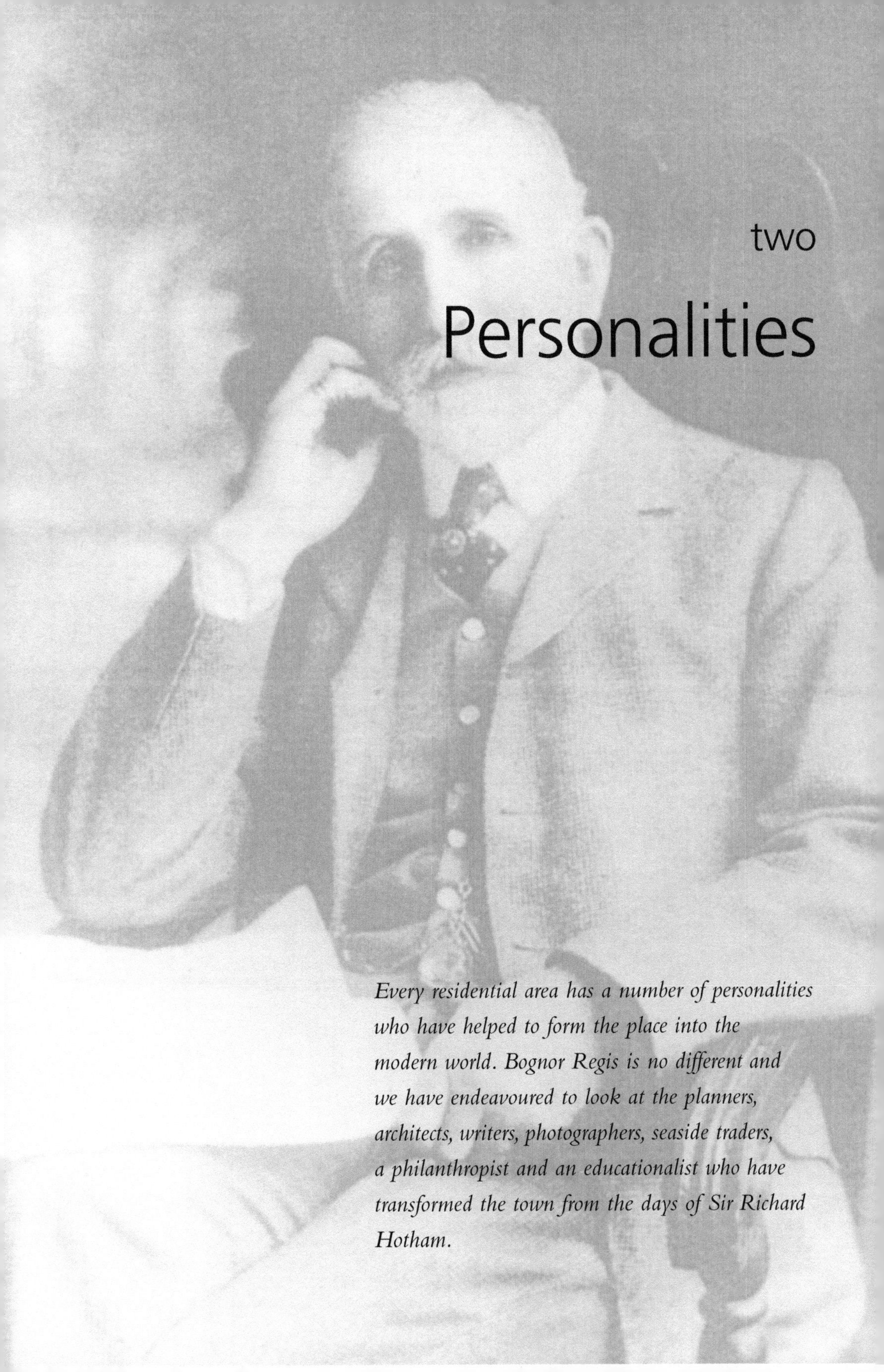

two

Personalities

Every residential area has a number of personalities who have helped to form the place into the modern world. Bognor Regis is no different and we have endeavoured to look at the planners, architects, writers, photographers, seaside traders, a philanthropist and an educationalist who have transformed the town from the days of Sir Richard Hotham.

William Tate was known as the 'Maker of Bognor' and was born in 1851. The family emigrated to Australia in 1868, returning in 1871. William started his building business in West Street and from 1900 he built the Princess Mary Memorial Home, the Arcade in 1902 and the Kursaal. He also erected the seafront railings and finally, many housing estates around the town. He was chairman of the Urban District Council until he died in 1931 aged eighty-one.

Henry Leopold Foster Guermonprez was born in 1858. He was well known as a skilled taxidermist and his work as a botanist was mentioned within *Flora of Sussex*.

He was involved in the discovery of the remains of a thirteenth-century chapel at Manor Farm, Nyetimber – now Barton Manor. He was also involved in the finding of ninety Bronze Age axes or *palstaves*, within Marshall Avenue. He died in 1924.

Gerard Young was born in 1912. He became a theatre critic and moved to Flansham in 1938. He became known for his books about his cottage and Flansham. In 1956 he joined the *Bognor Post* and developed his column and became our first journalist local historian. His book, *The History of Bognor*, finished by his brother, Derek after his death in 1972, is used as a basis for local research today.

E. Martin Venables was born in 1901 and his family moved to No. 3 Marine Parade in 1905. He was an amateur geologist and natural historian who lived in West Bognor for much of his life and died in 1990. He wrote the *Selborne Notes* in the *West Sussex Gazette* for over fifty years. He discovered a fossil insect fauna in the London Clay, over 50 million years old and his work gave the names *Bognoria* and *Aldwickia* to fossil plants. *Venablesia*, a wood-boring fossil beetle was named after him.

Samuel Reynolds was born at Thaxted, Essex on 3 May 1847. The son of a farmer, he obtained his cabinet-making indentures prior to coming to Bognor around 1867 where he founded his business in West Street as a cabinet maker. His philosophy was to offer his customers quality goods and personal service. This policy has paid dividends and been handed down through the generations up to the present day. Samuel died in 1897.

Joscelyn Reginald Hansford, seen here in his Masonic regalia, was born in 1881 and had by the age of twenty-seven purchased his first shop. He did not use the word 'sell' but preferred 'serve' instead. He served the community and became a founder member of the Chamber of Trade, Bognor Bowls Club and his interest in the Bognor Hospital resulted in the formation of the town's ambulance service. He was also involved in the town's improvement committee.

Frederick Jenkins moved to Bognor in 1886 from Eastbourne with his wife, to begin building a business in Longford Road. Their wedding present from her father was a fleet of bathing machines which they painted in blue and white stripes. His haulage business was near the station in a road to be named Longford Road, which he built at a cost of £700.

Mary Wheatland was the only personality in the town's history to be depicted on postcards. Mary saved over thirty lives and was decorated by the Royal Humane Society. Her bathing machine station on the east of the pier was shown on numerous picture postcards. Mary was born on 16 August 1835 in Aldingbourne, married in 1857 to George Wheatland and died in 1924 at the age of eighty-nine, leaving memories for all who met her.

Billy Butlin became associated with Bognor Regis in 1931 when he opened his amusement park on the corner of Lennox Street. As a generous man, he provided funds to local schools, organisations and charities. He stayed here to oversee the building of the holiday camp which opened on 2 July 1960. It covered 58 acres and cost an estimated £25 million. He was knighted in July 1964 for his charity work. He died in June 1980.

Ron Whittington was born in 1917. He became a popular figure on the seafront until his death in 1989. His boats, deckchairs, miniature train and other concessions gave pleasure to thousands of visitors to the beach. He also became a school governor and a councillor as he felt passionately about the town he loved.

William Fletcher was the last private owner of Hotham Park House when he died in 1941 aged eighty-nine. William Fletcher had a school named after him and was a great financial benefactor to the town. On his death, there was insufficient money for a grave. This was rectified in 1980 when the Local History Society raised funds to place a headstone on his grave at North Mundham.

John Cyril Hawes was born in 1876 in Richmond and constructed the White Tower at No. 16 Aldwick Road. He became an Anglican priest and then joined the Catholic Church, travelling to Australia where he designed churches. He ultimately left the Church, becoming a recluse. He died in a Miami hospital on 26 June 1956. He was buried in a cave on Mount Alvernie. His work around the world has made him well known worldwide.

Henry Lovett started the *Bognor Observer* newspaper in Bognor in 1872. Henry was a man who had many projects on the go at the same time; chairman of the Bognor Laundry, chairman of the Bognor Gasworks, Treasurer of the Westhamptnett Union (the workhouse), chairman of Bognor Urban Council and a Justice of the Peace based at the County Court in Chichester. This influential and interesting character died on 3 May 1922.

Richard Sharp collected postage stamps and this formed the basis of his fame. In 1882 a customer bet Richard that he would not be able to cover part of a room with stamps within a time restriction. Richard took up this challenge – as anyone would – and with 76,795 stamps, he succeeded in covering all aspects of the room by sticking the stamps on all the walls and furniture and obviously won his bet.

three
Learning

Learning was carried out within churches as well as schools. At one time, there were reported to be over seventy-five schools and records have been sourced for over fifty locations of religious environments.

South Bersted church was consecrated in 1405, long before Bognor the modern seaside resort came into existence. It is here that many town notables are buried including Sir Richard Hotham, Mary Wheatland and William Hardwicke. An altar screen contains an illuminated screen showing the Ten Commandments. South Bersted School and church hall are situated adjacent, providing village facilities.

The first St John's church was opened in 1822 in the Steyne, backing on to Market Street, but closed in 1891 due to lack of space. The new church, namely St John's, London Road was opened in 1886 and was large enough for a congregation of 1,000. The church closed in 1972 due to falling numbers. Also in the picture is the Water Tower situated near the bend of London Road, now demolished.

The congregational first place of worship in Bognor was in Chichester Road near today's hospital. They moved to this site on the corner of London Road and High Street in newly constructed premises in 1869 where they remained until 1929. Due to the noise of the traffic they sold their site to Timothy Whites and moved to Linden Road, where they remain today as the United Reformed church.

St Wilfrid's church was dedicated in 1910 and operational although the original tin church was still in evidence. The church was never finished as per the original design of a bell tower and two further bays with a west baptistery. However this has not detracted from the fact that this church is now the Parish Church of Bognor Regis.

Above: The Revd Mosse was asked by the Bishop of Chichester to commence a new parish in Aldwick due to the influx of people between Bognor Regis and Pagham. The original cost of the land was £525. St Richard's church in Gossamer Lane was consecrated on 12 May 1934 and would appear to be one of the last traditional looking structures built in Bognor Regis.

Above: The Servite Convent in Hawthorn Road opened in 1888 until it closed in 1974. It was designed by Mr J.A. Hansom who was the designer of the well-known Hansom Cabs. It was demolished in 1975, allowing Servite Close housing to be constructed and opened in 1977. The small convent cemetery is still in existence. It is interesting to surmise the purpose of postcards showing the inside of the convent – since it was a closed order.

Opposite below: This ornate chapel was in the grounds of St Michael's School, Upper Bognor Road and used by the school until they evacuated in 1941. The St Michael's building was taken over in 1946 as part of an emergency teacher training college. The chapel has since been used as a dining hall and is now the reprographic department of Chichester University, Bognor campus.

The Servite Fathers were invited to England from Italy in 1864 by Cardinal Wiseman to establish a foundation in Fulham, London. Within sixteen years, they were invited to establish their second foundation in Clarence Road, Bognor. A formal opening for Our Lady of Seven Dolours was held on 16 August 1882, although the church was incomplete. In 1957 the work was completed and they held another official opening on 1 November.

"O enter then His gates with praise,
Approach with joy His courts unto."

Once referred to as the smallest church in Bognor Regis, St Peter's church in Frith Road was dedicated by the Rt Revd George Bell on 23 August 1939. Within ten days war was declared and the council took over the premises to cater for the influx of evacuees. Eventually it returned to Church use until 1977, when plans were made for its demolition and homes built on the site.

Whilst being a modern picture of the Salvation Army church, its original site was in Scott Street until it moved into these premises vacated by the Bognor Baptists' church who moved to Victoria Drive. Both of these churches continue education of a religious nature and work within the communities into the twenty-first century.

Education within churches took many forms and here we can see the Boys Brigade of 1933-34 who were connected to the United Reformed church in Linden Road. The Boy Scouts, Girl Guides and other such groups continued with education by providing life skills to the younger members of the churches.

This picture appears in a 1912 advertisement for the Royal Naval Academy which was situated in Victoria Drive, in conjunction with Holyrood School. There were many schools throughout the town which specialised in preparing young men for entry into the Royal Navy.

SPACIOUS GYMNASIUM

LARGE GARDEN with TENNIS COURTS

Courtfield House School for Girls
VICTORIA DRIVE, BOGNOR

PREMISES SPECIALLY CONSTRUCTED FOR A SCHOOL. SANITATION MODERN. HOT WATER HEATING THROUGHOUT. CLASS ROOMS, LARGE, AIRY AND WELL LIGHTED. PREPARATION FOR PUBLIC EXAMINATIONS.

FEES FROM 60 GUINEAS ∴ PRINCIPALS: **MISS WALL & MISS SCOTT**

This school advertisement of 1912 shows both a girls' boarding school and a day school for the daughters of gentlemen. Operating in Victoria Drive from 1912, it continued until 1940, when it was evacuated to Monmouthshire. The school was later purchased by WH Smith for a staff convalescent home, and renamed Hambledon Place. It was demolished and replaced by a modern housing development.

HOLYROOD SCHOOL
BOGNOR

Telegrams: "Holyrood, Bognor"
Telephone: Bognor 65

Headmasters:
B. C. BRODIE, M.C., B.A., Eton and Magdalen College, Oxford.
L. T. PROSSER EVANS, Llandovery and Keble College, Oxford
(Late Lecturers in Modern History at the Royal Military College, Sandhurst).

Holyrood School successfully prepares boys from 7-14 years for the Public Schools and entry into the Royal Navy. From 1919-1927 thirteen Scholarships have been gained at the Public Schools, eighty-nine boys have passed the Common Entrance Examination and five boys have entered the R.N.C., Dartmouth.

Special attention is paid to Diet. Vegetables and Fresh Fruit are included throughout the year ॐ Grade "A" Milk only is used.

Miniature Rifle Range. Chapel. Handicraft Room. Kitchen & Flower Gardens. Library. Recreation Room. Sanatorium (detached). Gymnasium. Sea Bathing (Private).

The extensive Grounds and Playing Field provide ample space for Cricket, Football (Association & Rugby) and Tennis. Badminton is played in the Gymnasium.

(Arrangements can be made for placing, during holidays, boys whose parents are abroad).

Page 96

Holyrood School in Victoria Drive opened in 1889 and was specially designed with 7 acres of playing fields. It was noted for its magnificent collection of local fossils including old Bognor rock and Sussex Iron with some of the exhibits found in Victoria Drive. Denis Thatcher was a pupil here in the 1920s. This 1928 advertisement shows the range of activities available. Later the school became Streete Court School and is now converted into flats.

This view of Aspley House, Barrack Lane, Aldwick is depicted within a 1950s advertisement for the girls' school. Pupils receive the 'most careful home training, importance being attached to physical development and to the formation of character'.

Pupils at Lyon Street School expressing their enjoyment of school. Sadly these photographs are more often than not undated, without the names of the pupils. In 2006 this type of classroom photograph is no longer taken as a reminder of school days.

St Michael's School, Upper Bognor Road, Bognor Regis was formerly known as Arran Lodge and then Lennox Lodge. The premise became St Michael's School for Girls in around 1856 and was known as the most exclusive girls' school in Bognor when it charged fifty guineas per term in 1938. In 1941 the pupils were evacuated to Penzance.

A most important subject to be taught to young ladies was cookery as shown in this school photograph. This picture is taken from St Michael's school prospectus, c. 1910.

The Government set up the Emergency Teacher Training Scheme in 1946 which offered a one-year teacher training course, because of the shortage of teachers after the war. A high percentage of the students were recently demobbed from the services. This photograph shows students on the rural studies course learning the art of bee keeping at the Bognor Regis Teacher Training College.

This opening ceremony was on 23 May 1939. By 1959 it had been named William Fletcher School and in May 1960 it became the Bognor Grammar School. In 2006 it is the Bognor Regis Community College where the campus provides facilities from nursery provision through to adult education and fitness. This is a long way from the 'three Rs' originally taught in schools.

four
Living

The development of any location requires building materials and an increasing population and thus this area was able to comply. One of the things that Sir Richard Hotham found was that the local clay was suitable for brick making. Development since the 1800s has continued and therefore we have endeavoured to include a range of properties from various eras and styles. In the twenty-first century many homes are built within housing complexes as opposed to the individual homes built in the past.

Valhalla is one of three houses which originally formed Russell Place in the High Street. Valhalla and Manora were built around 1820 and remain as two of the few remaining examples of Regency architecture. The third house, built around 1790, was demolished in 1939 when Lyon Street was widened. 'Valhalla' was rented by Frederick Dadswell from 1860 as a holiday retreat from London. He retired here in 1890 and the house still remains with the same family.

Albert Terrace, in the foreground on the right, is thought to have been built around 1861. This bow-fronted terrace in the High Street was originally seen as a quiet residential area. Trade came when Ezra Royston moved from West Street to Albert Terrace in the 1870s and opened the first shop selling footwear and clothing.

Glamis Street, showing Beaumont Terrace on the right, 1893. Other sections were known as Queens Square, Strathmore Gardens, Lyon Villas and Denmark Terrace.

Leonard House is shown on the Ordnance Survey of 1875 surrounded by fields and appeared to be at the wrong angle to the main London Road. It is opposite the current town library. Though it was once owned by a fruiterer, this house has had a chequered career. Lately it has been used as flats and a nursing home and currently there is a query over demolition.

This family gathering is outside No. 5 Gainsboro Road in the centre of Bognor. It was given to us by the late Mr Homer whose family is in this picture. In the 1980s we resided at No. 4 Gainsboro Road for a number of years. These town centre small cottages were in cul-de-sacs off Ockley Road, originally known as Circus Street.

Sudley Road was built in 1878 across meadows; it contains a number of interesting and historical buildings. It was originally named to commemorate the 3rd Earl of Arran, Viscount Sudley of Gore, who for a number of years was a landowner in Bognor. On the east side is the Bognor Club which was erected in 1837 as the Assembly Rooms for the town.

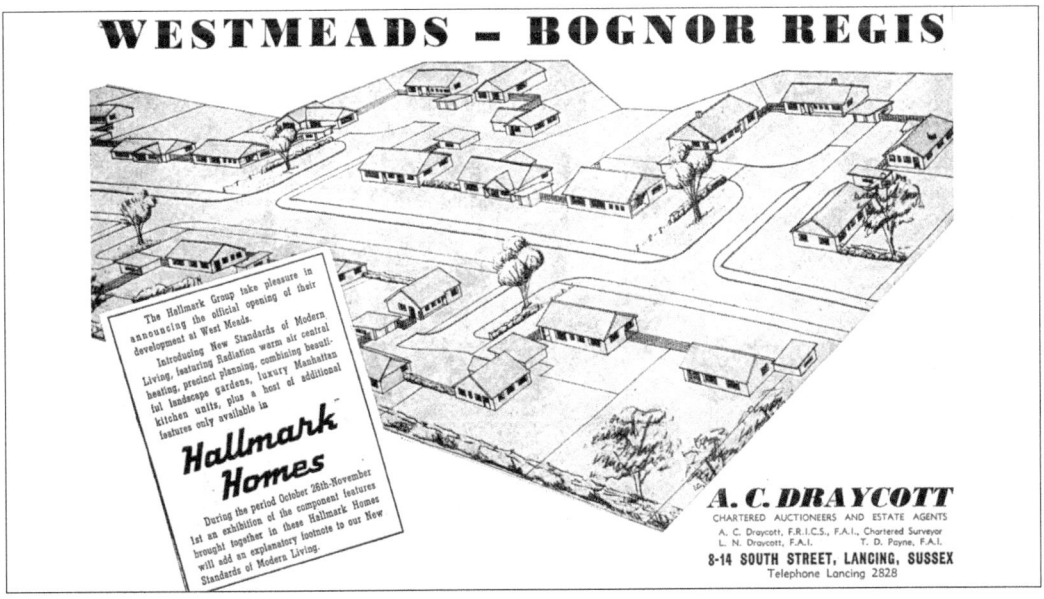

The West Meads Estate was built in 1961 and claimed to be the 'largest single area of development in West Sussex'. The 130-acre site of West Meads contained over 700 bungalows. In the centre there were twelve retail shops with car parking beside a community centre and church. The church closed in December 2006. The area was previously farm land and during 1944/5 was used as the Bognor Advanced Landing Ground prior to D-Day.

East View Cottage in the High Street was built by William Collis around 1815 and he lived there until his death in 1860 aged ninety-eight years. His family continued to reside there and his grandson visited in 1868 on a painting holiday. William painted at least seven scenes from the cottage windows and garden which provide us with an excellent insight into that area of the town.

The Steyne (c. 1900) was developed in the 1820s. Bath House was built by James Smith in 1824 as the only public establishment in the town where you could get a cheap hot bath. The Primitive Methodist church operated here opposite St John's Chapel of Ease, built in 1821 by Daniel Wonham. The central garden area was for use by the residents of the Steyne and in 1872 the iron railings were erected to retain privacy.

The White Tower is a unique building which was erected by John Cyril Hawes and is still a landmark on Aldwick Road which was originally called Culver Street. John personally carved with a penknife two brackets which he used to support the flat hood over the front door. He also designed houses in Victoria Road and Swansea Gardens in addition to churches in Australia and elsewhere.

"Paradise," Dark Lane, Aldwick: destroyed by fire, c.1909

From an original drawing by E M. Venables, based on a photo (EMV) of an oil painting owned by the late Mr. Walter Finch of High House, Hawthorn Road, Aldwick

This unique idea was achieved in 1938 by Arthur Winham, a speculative builder from London – an estate of 104 flats, built in 26 blocks over a 6.75-acre site. Their rental was £100 per annum. These Japanese Gardens were created by Seyemon Kusomoto FRHS, a well-known Japanese landscape artist, and they echoed the famous Silver Pavilion Gardens in Kyoto, Japan. Sadly they were demolished but today's homes constructed in 1977 retain the name.

Opposite above: Paradise Cottage was built around 1802 and called Aldwick Villa, being the indulgence of Sir Thomas Brooke Pechell. By 1852 Revd Thomas Scutt had bought the property and renamed it Paradise. A guide book of the time described it as a 'pretty thatched cottage with a veranda and pillars clothed with jasmine, honeysuckle and fragrant shrubs'. Sadly it was destroyed by fire in April 1909.

Opposite below: Mr Donald Dalrymple bought the grounds of Paradise in 1929 for £3,000 and spent £30,000 constructing a house in a Dutch Moorish design for which he brought in Spanish builders. The two large domes weighed more than ten tons each. He named the house Strange Gardens House. It is believed because the garden was strange in that it was below beach level.

In 1887 the *Kelly's Directory of Sussex* reported a new development of 'several fine residences being erected, in Victoria Drive of more than a mile in length … planted with trees on either side, forming an extremely pleasant boulevard'. One of these is St Leonard's Lodge, No. 123 Victoria Drive which was built in 1907. By the late 1960s it was converted into a nursing home, which still remains in 2007.

The Newtown Estate in North Bersted was built in the 1930s by G.A. Neal & Sons comprising six roads, Central Avenue, South Way, Central Drive, Newtown Avenue and Greencourt Drive. Along the Chichester Road were shops and a social club. No more than ten houses were built to the acre and front elevations varied. This 2000 photograph of a pair of semis shows they have hardly altered in the seventy years since they were built.

Fitzleet House was developed and built by Bernard Sunley between 1959 and 1962. He was considered the youngest and probably the most far-sighted of the small and powerful group of construction millionaires who were rebuilding Britain in the sixties. When opened by the Duke of Richmond, he remarked that 'Bognor had vision to build this new high construction'. The top of the building is the site of the weather statistics recording equipment.

A photograph of the Linden (Self Build) Housing Association Limited shown outside their Pevensey Road site, c. 1964. From left to right: Norman Saunders, Tom Gillespie, Norman Smith, David Rogers, Ian Baker, Peter Langridge, Bob Bradford, Brian Simpson, Ken Burns, Brian Hamer, Ken Hawkins and Malcolm Riggs. Self-built homes came into being because a wage of between £11 and £14 per week was insufficient to raise a mortgage. The men continued with their full-time employment.

This is a 1934 plan for a chalet bungalow in Hillsboro Road. This was at a time of expansion for the building of houses, bungalows and shops in Bognor Regis following the visit of King George V. This has been our home for over twenty years.

five
Shopping

The shopping experience has changed over the years from the corner shop to the 'out of town' experience. Within any location it is possible for the shopping centre to move and here in Bognor Regis it was in West Street, before the development of the town when the High Street and London Road became the town centre.

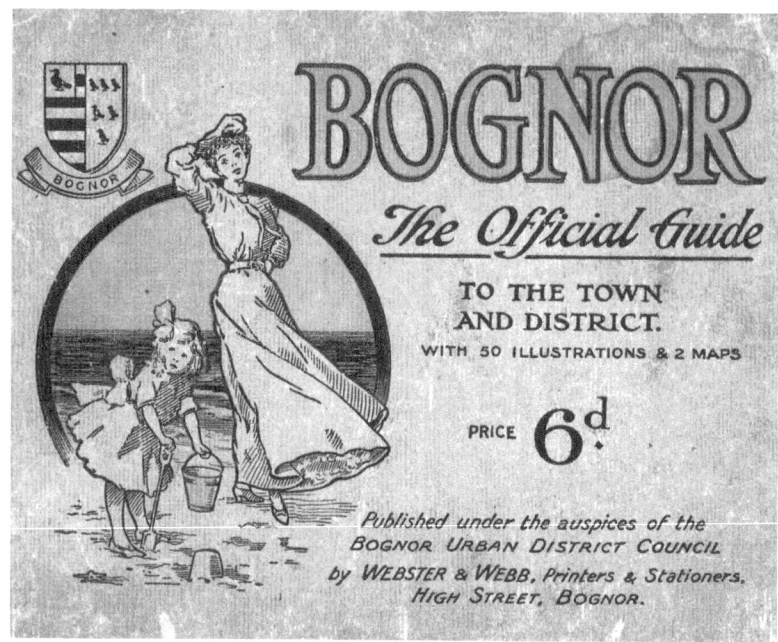

This official 1912 Guide is just one of a large number that were produced to advertise both the town and the surrounding area and also the various traders who provided such a wide range of services. These books are invaluable to local historians.

Buckle & Clidero

HIGH-CLASS GROCERS
WINE, SPIRIT AND
BEER MERCHANTS

TEAS, COFFEES, GROCERIES
PROVISIONS, FRUIT &
BOTTLED BEERS

Special Value in all Departments. Unrivalled Quality. Competitive Prices.
Telephone No. 33 P.O.

A House Agency Department is also conducted in connection with the Stores. Special attention given to all enquiries.

23 High St., Bognor

Buckle & Clidero operated from No. 23 High Street and were under the personal supervision of A. Clidero from 1896. This advertisement from the 1912 *Guide* describes the services offered. In 1953 they were bought out by the Roberts chain of off-licenses. Interestingly these premises have continued to offer wine, spirits and provisions into 2007.

Staley's was founded in 1888 by George Whittle Staley when he opened his ladies' costumiers' shop at No. 25 High Street. Ralph Staley, son of the founder, operated the company from 1914 until its closure in 1958. The business expanded and eventually moved into new premises on the corner of London Road as shown below.

In 1914 Staley's and adjacent shops were built in the long tea gardens of Camden House and were called the London Road Buildings. Camden House shown here on the right was demolished in the mid-1930s to enable Staley's to expand. The company sold out to Bobby's in 1959, a family firm who operated until it was acquired in 2000 by the local company of Reynolds. In 2007 it is operated by Bon Marché.

OPENING FRIDAY, JULY 24

MARKS AND SPENCER LTD.
NEW SUPER STORE AT
4 LONDON ROAD, BOGNOR

Make a note of the opening date and be one of the first to see Bognor's latest and most up-to-date store. Here you will find a wonderful variety of merchandise for the family and the home — all of thoroughly reliable quality. There is no secret about the astonishingly low prices. They are simply the result of Marks and Spencer's policy of buying in large quantities from the leading British manufacturers. Your money will go further at Marks and Spencer's, the store where you will always find quality and value.

- NOTHING OVER 5/- • 90% BRITISH GOODS •
Ladies' and Children's Drapery • Men's and Boys' Wear • Hosiery • Footwear • Fancy Goods • Toilet • Confectionery • Canned Goods and Fresh Fruits • Toys • Lighting, etc.

ASK FOR PARTICULARS OF OUR WEEKLY CLUBS

When 'Marks and Spencer Ltd.' opened on Friday 24 July 1936 in London Road on the site of Ivy Lodge, it was an extremely modern building in comparison to the much smaller shops in the road. When they opened, staff welfare was a high priority and the maximum working week was forty-eight hours. Staff could obtain a hot dinner for 6d. Marks & Spencer left this site in August 1990.

The High Street Art Deco Southdown's bus station was built in 1934. Buses ceased to operate from around 1980 although the façade remained for many years. Two adjacent shops seen above were the Co-op and Cleeves the chemist, who produced numerous postcards of the town and surrounding area.

Harry Mann had a very novel way to ensure people knew where his drapers and milliners shop was situated, without using the street name or number, as shown in this 1912 advertisement.

Today above the modern shop fronts of Nobles Amusements and First Choice can still be seen the original building as shown in this photograph. Either side are modern buildings, although there are still other original buildings in London Road, which are visible if you look above the shop fronts.

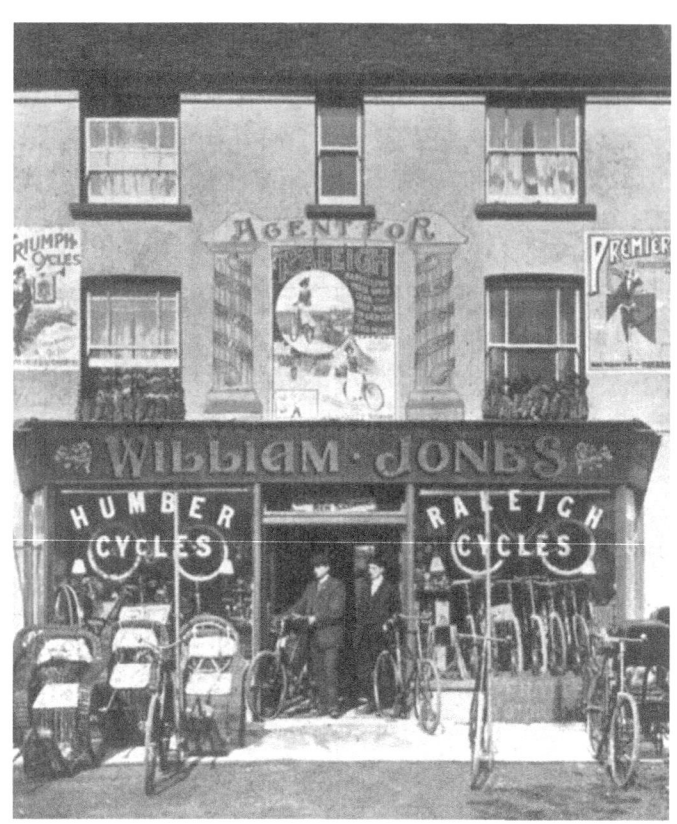

Left: The site of the first business which was to develop into Jones' Garage and to exist in the town for over 100 years. It was opened by William Jones in 1902 on the corner of High Street and Bedford Street. The shop at No. 58 was set back from the main road and demolished to make way for the Citizens Regency Building Society. In 2007 it is the Portman Building Society.

Below: Goodacres shop stood on the corner of the Esplanade and York Road from the 1920s until 1972. Remembered mainly as a toy shop, it also sold leather and fancy goods and advertised as a tobacconist and stationers. The building was demolished along with the Rex and other buildings to make way for the regeneration of that part of the seafront.

Above: Joscelyn Hansford was working as the branch manager of an outfitter, when asked if he wanted to purchase a till from a trader who was closing. He replied 'yes' to the till and took the shop, paying a guinea per week. Thus, Hansford realised the opening of his first shop. He moved across the road to new premises and also acquired the Congregational Institute in 1931, which was set back from the road. He built his third shop in front of the institute which had a very imposing facade, considered by many to be years ahead of its time.

Below: This 1959 photograph shows the interior of Hansford's third shop in London Road. Their attention to detail was such that they dipped hundreds of ties into a vat of black dye for the funeral of King George V. The company is still in existence today in Chichester, providing that 'old style service'.

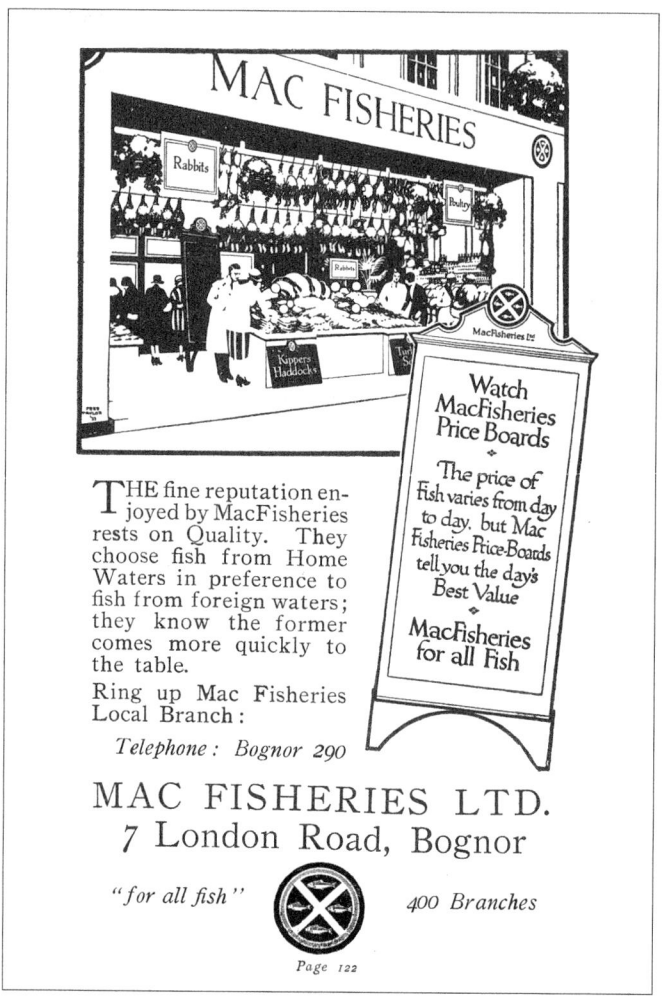

By the end of the 1920s Mac Fisheries shops were opening in many towns as outlets for the Scottish fishing trade. Bognor was no different and in around 1925 Mac Fisheries opened at No. 7 London Road and remained trading for almost fifty years.

Above: This picture shows the shops built by Arthur Cox: Lemmon drapers at No. 1, Gear tailors at No. 3 and Hubbards, ironmongers at No. 5. This premise of Lemmon's was in the High Street near the site of today's post office. Frank Lemmon commenced his business in 1903 with this drapers shop. In 1914 they moved to larger premises in London Road. Eventually they were purchased by Woolworth's in 1960.

Right: There was a fire in the Arcade in 1930 and all the shops had to find temporary premises whilst repair work was completed. Freeman, Hardy & Willis was one of these shops. They moved into No. 11 High Street premises built and owned by Arthur Cox, prior to their return to the Arcade.

Above: The Parfrements store opened as a butchers and poulterers at Nos 49/49a High Street in 1923, having purchased the business from Mr Cheney. From 1929, they advertised as being exclusive purveyors to the Royal Table at Craigweil House. The building with its beautifully tiled walls was demolished in 1970 to make way for a more modern style of shop, which opened as Gamley's.

Left: Ethel and Olive Carter, two of four sisters who ran a wool and art needlework depot originally based in the Arcade but which moved to No. 51 High Street in 1925. In 2007 the shop is 'Pick a Wish' convenience stores and off-license. On the side wall above the roof line of the adjacent shop, it is still possible to see the advertisement for E. & O. Carter.

Look above the shop front and you can see the upper storey and roof of the original residence, Dorset Lodge. People still remember the aromas that they encountered upon entering Isted's store. The building was demolished and replaced with the northern side of Woolworth's.

The Reynolds' furnishing business was founded by Samuel Reynolds in 1867 in West Street. Three years later he moved to No. 29 High Street and was joined by his brother, Arthur. They then extended into No. 27 and finally No. 31 was taken over for the undertaking side of the business. Their advertising included, 'Auctioneers, Appraisers, House Agents, Cabinet Makers, Upholsterers and Undertakers'. This picture shows the building in 1939. Today Samuel's descendants still operate the business making them the longest established family business in the town.

This advertisement is taken from a 1926 town guide.

In 1804 George Field opened a butcher's shop in Swansea Lodge, West Street. He moved the business across the road to No. 33 in 1853 where the Field family continued to trade until 1949 when they sold it to Sid Rishman. No. 33 continued as a butcher's shop until 1997 under different owners, but always retained the Field name. Following its transformation into a private home the Field tiles have been retained.

Above: Frank Lalouette was born in 1901 and died in 1969. He opened his own photography shop at No. 32 West Street around 1930 and sold the business when he retired in 1955. Frank was the official photographer in the district for the Ministry of Information and his photos of blitzed Bognor, crashed aircraft, Allied troops etc. provide local historians with a very good insight into Bognor Regis during the war.

The Co-operative Store in Canada Grove

The Centre For Pure Foods in Bognor Regis

The spacious modern premises of the Portsea Island Co-operative Society in Canada Grove have rapidly become the centre for all those who wish to be sure they are obtaining the highest quality foods at keen prices.

The enormous weekly sales are a guarantee that stocks are always fresh and in the finest possible condition, and the Society's definite policy is to sell at the keenest possible prices for the high quality offered.

By the way, membership is entirely free. Why not obtain particulars?

DEPARTMENTS:
GROCERY & PROVISIONS   CONFECTIONERY & PASTRY
BUTCHERY & COOKED MEATS   TOBACCO & CIGARETTES

ORDERS COLLECTED AND DELIVERED FREE
TO ALL PARTS OF THE DISTRICT
FULL DIVIDEND GIVEN

PORTSEA ISLAND MUTUAL
CO-OPERATIVE
SOCIETY LTD.
CANADA GROVE (facing Pavilion Gardens), BOGNOR REGIS
Regd. Office: 48, St. Mary's Road, Portsmouth

Above: This descriptive advertisement was in the 1937 *Town Guide*. The first PIMCO (Portsea Island Mutual Co-operative Society) opened in Bognor Regis in 1933 and was situated at Canada Grove and the company still has a number of shops around the town. Wartime advertising quotes branches at North Bersted and Hawthorn Road. In the 1950s they expanded with two shops in the High Street but these ceased as 'out of town' shopping became popular.

Oppoosite below: Herbert S. Gales here at No. 57 High Street and later at No. 4 York Road where his name is still tiled in the doorway in 2006. He traded as general and fancy drapers in addition to being an 'outfitter and shoe warehouse'. He advertised as being the 'cheapest house for mourning' in Bognor.

The Tuck Shop was a surviving part of a farmhouse dating back to the mid-1700s. Mr Munday, a cobbler, once lived there and it is alleged that Princess Victoria purchased her first pair of boots from there. This picture shows Robin Bradley aged six and Carol Bradley aged four deciding what to purchase around 1949. This building was demolished in 1968 for a road widening scheme which never materialised.

HIGH STREET, BOGNOR

Above: In 1929 Timothy Whites purchased this site on the corner of London Road and the High Street for £17,000 from the Congregational church and there was a provision that no alcohol was to be sold on the site. After moving here from the Arcade, they eventually moved in with Boots the chemist in London Road before ultimately closing down as a company. Today it is the Abbey.

Right: This sketch card shows a small corner of Bognor. It is Little High Street which runs from Waterloo Square through to the High Street. In the centre of the sketch is Gough's the art shop that existed on this site from 1912 to 2002.

Above: Mr A.R.P. Olby founded his business in Penge in 1878. His first store in Bognor was established in 1927 in Gravits Lane and by 1928 he took over a railway wharf at the station yard, within the railway station boundary wall.

Above: The House of Hawkes was established in 1872 and was a prominent store at No. 9 High Street. This is the cover of one of their catalogues which not only lists all items available but the prices as well. There are many pages of handy hints to help the customer. I have been told of customers arriving and being provided with a glass of sherry whilst they discussed their order prior to its delivery.

Opposite below: In 1941 Olby's opened an ironmongers shop at No. 7 High Street. By 1954 they had taken over No. 11 and in 1972 No. 9 had been included to form the large High Street departmental store remembered by so many. Sadly in 1984 the store was closed due partly to a decline in this type of operation.

Left: The Misses Gray ran a woollen and knitted goods shop from this site from the 1920s up until around 1936. They converted the ground floor into a café which remained there for the next thirty years. In 1955 the Merchant Taylor's Convalescent Home was replaced with the Queensway and Pricerite supermarket. In 1963 the developers purchased and demolished Polly Anne's to extend the supermarket up to the bus station.

Below: Macari's first ice cream parlour was opened on the Esplanade on the Queen's Coronation Day, 2 June 1953 by Saverio Macari. In 1957 he had purchased the Esplanade Theatre Café and Hotham Park Café. He sold the Esplanade site in 1961 and opened his London Road shop in 1962. His sons and daughter now manage other shops in the South of England, with Enzo managing the Bognor Regis shop.

six
Recreation

The recreational facilities within the area have been enjoyed by both residents and visitors. Enjoyment in our spare time was the key to this chapter.

Above: As a twelve-year-old boy, Trevor Jennings performing a Punch & Judy show at a VE Day party in Orchard Way. Trevor had made his début as a Punch & Judy puppeteer two and a half years earlier on 5 January 1943. This was held at the Bognor Regis Baptist church in Canada Grove. Trevor is still entertaining children today at public events and private parties.

Opposite above: Bathing machines formed an integral part of the town's seaside heritage. Machine No. 23, on the right, is still in existence in 2006. Mr Jenkins had over 150 machines and would use his horses on 1 June annually to move them from Shripney down to the beach.

Opposite below: These three children, Jimmy, Dick and Daphne seem to be enjoying Bognor beach in 1921 and certainly depict a typical seaside scene enjoyed by so many visitors to the town. In the background can be seen the steps leading up to the bathing huts that were along the Esplanade near the junction of Clarence Road.

Above: Roller skating was very popular on the pier in the 1900s. This picture shows Hilda Beaton, a well-known personality of the time, in the middle of the picture and the pier master on the right.

Left: The Pavilion entertainment complex commenced its life as an aircraft hangar for the Norman Thompson Flight Co. Ltd in Middleton-on-Sea. From 1919, at its new town centre site, it provided a wide range of entertainment and was said to have one of the best dance floors in the town, where many local people met their partners. It was also a favourite location for dances during the war and was frequented by service personnel.

Above: This 1926 photograph of the restaurant adjacent to the Pavilion shows the distinctive Lloyd Loom style furniture which only adds to this peaceful afternoon tea scene.

Right: The photograph of these two unnamed ladies was found within a personal 1900 photo album. It was in 1899 that mixed bathing was permitted on our beaches and perhaps they were beginning to enjoy the relaxation of these seaside rules.

Above: Billy Butlin brought entertainment to Bognor Regis in 1931 with a recreational centre on the promenade and corner of Lennox Street. Around the top of the building was emblazoned 'Our True Intent is all for your Delight'. It housed a 26-car dodgem track, a mirror maze, rifle range, juvenile ride, laughing clowns, Housey Housey and the largest display of coin slot machines seen on the coast at that time.

Left: A zoo and aquarium was opened by Billy Butlin in 1933 further west along the promenade. It was entered through a high rock façade as shown in the picture. Advertising claimed that black, brown and polar bears were to be seen alongside leopards, hyenas, pelicans, kangaroos and monkeys. A special attraction was 'Togo the Snake King' who gave frequent shows in the snake pit erected in the centre of the zoo.

Butlin's at BOGNOR

BUTLIN'S LTD., Great Britain's Greatest Holiday Caterers, of Skegness, Marblethorpe, Southsea, Felixstowe, Littlehampton, Clacton, Hayling Island, Hunstanton, etc. Have UP-TO-DATE AMUSEMENTS on the SEA FRONT at BOGNOR, including Dodgem Cars and Zoo

rganisers of Choir, Staff or School Outings contemplating a visit to BOGNOR, should write the General Manager of Butlin's Ltd., Grand Parade, Skegness, for particulars of half price concessions for Bognor Amusements.

HURRAH! ITS *Butlin's*
AMUSEMENT PARK ON THE SEA FRONT.

Proprietors of the £100,000 Luxury Holiday Camps at Skegness and Clacton-on-Sea

An advertisement of 1933 in the *Bognor Regis Post*, when Billy Butlin was first making his name in the entertainment world. 'Hurrah! It's Butlin's', became one of the catch phrases of the day. Another new initiative was to have all his employees in the amusement park dressed in white jackets with a red 'B' on the pocket.

BUTLIN'S
Typical Lounge Cafe and Heated Indoor Pool

One of the features of the holiday centres was their indoor swimming pools. Many local people learnt their swimming skills at the holiday centre. The pools had very large glass sides which would allow the swimmers to look out into the adjoining coffee lounges, causing great enjoyment.

Town Guides in the 1950s showed various activities that were available to the visitor. These pedal cars would be a welcome sight to children and allow fathers to relive their dreams as their children raced across the beach.

The Esplanade Theatre started life as a small bandstand but was eventually constructed into a theatre in 1937 at a cost of £3,666. It was one of the main entertainment centres and attracted all the main stars of the era. Finally in 1980 it was closed and demolished. Entertainment then continued in the newly constructed Regis Centre complex along the Esplanade.

The Beach and Esplanade (East of Pier), Bognor

A typical early twentieth-century seafront postcard view of the town showing the various beach activities available to the visitor. There were a large number of shops and traders involved in the postcard trade prior to the Second World War. This used postcard was imprinted with 'W.P. Marsh, Bognor' who was just one of the many postcard producers in the town.

The Kursaal building was constructed in 1910 and eventually changed its name to the Rex Building. It contained a cinema, theatre, shops and other entertainments. Eventually it was closed and demolished in May 1975 to enable the Regis Centre to be built and opened in 1980.

The Darcia band had this postcard produced, no doubt to advertise their services. This picture is of the bandstand east of the pier in front of the Royal Norfolk Hotel.

The Whittington family operated various sea trips during the summer. From left to right: Ron Whittington, Ken Court, Chris Palmer, Dave Fellick Snr and his daughter, Avril.

Pat Fossey aged four years and her sister Christine aged six years, enjoying a ride on Muffin the Mule in 1957. Muffin was a very popular children's television character of the period and was situated on the Esplanade, possibly in the area of the Rex Building, York Road.

These trampolines were operational in the 1970s beside the pier in front of Waterloo Square, an area engulfed by the newly constructed sea wall.

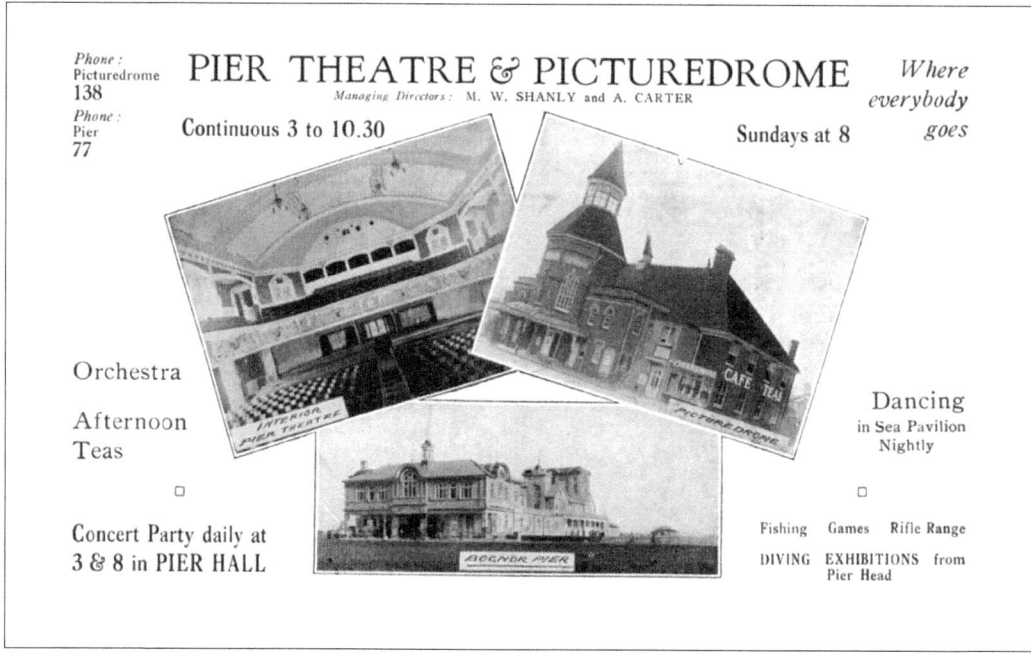

A posed photograph of the fishermen and seafront traders in front of the pier. Mary Wheatland, bathing machine proprietress can be seen in the centre. Note that concerts were held three times a day.

This advertisement from the 1930s shows the joint operation of the Pier Theatre and the Picturedrome which provided much-enjoyed cinema and shows for the holiday makers. Of course, residents also enjoyed the benefits of the stars who frequented these major entertainment complexes at the time.

78

The Bognor Bowls Club was formed in 1923 following the construction of the first bowling green and pavilion in Waterloo Square. This postcard view also shows the Bognor Regis Methodist church which was opened in 1926. Bowls is still actively played on this site today.

Uncle George Edgar's Thespian Concert Parties were just one of the seaside entertainments that operated on the beach in front of the Royal Hotel. This postcard was photographed by W.P. Marsh who became famous for his 'High Seas' pictures of Bognor.

The initial wooden construction which is shown in many of the Edwardian postcards is noted as being on the 'East Parade'. Unfortunately it was removed at the start of the Second World War to make way for gun emplacements. With the war over and everyone getting back into the holiday spirit, the council finally received their compensation in the sum of £538 from the War Department. The council then purchased this new bandstand from Cheltenham.

The pier opened 4 May 1865. In 1911 over £20,000 was spent to widen the shore end and include an arcade of twelve shops. There was a large theatre constructed seating 1,400 people. Storm damage in 1965 and 1999 has considerably reduced the length of the original pier. During the First World War it was used by the Army and in the Second World War it was used by the Navy as HMS St Barbara.

This Massey picture of children in the sea was taken around 1912 and clearly shows the Kursaal Building in the background. The children would have been photographed from a boat and are clearly dressed in their best clothes. They could possibly have arrived in the town on one of the numerous Sunday excursion trains. The photographs of D. Massey were also used by other postcard manufacturers including the 'LL' series of cards.

Frank Bale and his family came to live in Bognor in 1910 and entertained on the sands in the area in front of the Royal Hotel. He amused children with his clowning and juggling plus playing the banjo and guitar. The annual rental for his pitch was just £1. His daughter Vi assisted him, performing with the marionettes.

A typical seaside scene. The Ashton brothers were one of the main donkey ride operators on our seafront. At one time the donkey stand was on the Esplanade at its junction with York Road.

Here on the beach in the 1930s we see June Davis in the centre on one of the horses from the Captain Millard stable which was situated to the rear of the Royal Norfolk Hotel.

June Davis and her two friends enjoying a goat cart ride on Bognor beach in the 1930s. These rides cost 6d and were seen as more of a special treat than a donkey ride. To the right of the picture can be seen The Rex building with the pier in the background.

An even more luxurious ride was that of the carriage, seen here on the beach in front of Mary Wheatland's office and Butlin's Amusements.

Left: Hotham Park was opened to the public in 1947. In 1950 Pets Corner had been established and within five years over 1,106,000 people had visited this established venture. The 5.5-acre site contained a wide range of animals, from pigs to ducks, Spanish sheep to Chinese bantams. Families of animals were also on display within their own detached houses and grounds. Later it became known as Zootopia and in 1983 changed its name to Rainbow's End.

Below: Rainbow's End was a favourite with families but finally closed in 1998 and is currently derelict. However, the Hotham Park Heritage Trust has submitted plans for the creation of a leisure area back within the full confines of the park.

Right: Kay Smith on holiday in the mid-1960s, sitting beside Mickey Mouse. This was a very popular photo opportunity for people visiting Pets Corner in Hotham Park.

Below: Crowds being entertained by the folk dancers from the Bognor Regis Training College as part of the Festival of Britain celebrations on 27 June 1951. The audience were invited to join in the dancing.

Left: A busy seafront scene captured by a photographer in the 1960s. This picture shows fishermen's boats, a child with bucket and spade and the *Bluebird* which provided boat trips. In the background can be seen the paddle steamer at the pier landing stage.

Below: This picture shows the 1935 carnival procession. Note the writing on the float, which was a well-known phrase in advertising after King George V recuperated in Bognor in 1929 and then designated the addition of 'Regis' to the town name. Images of this event were produced on a series of *Carte Postale* postcards.

seven

Travel

Various methods have been used over the years to arrive at, and travel around any seaside resort. For many people, their first experience of the seaside was their annual Sunday school outing on a railway excursion.

In the twenty-first century it seems incredible that the closest local railway station, operating from 1846, was situated out at Woodgate, a journey of three miles from Bognor. On 1 June 1864 a new station was opened in Bognor.

Following the long wait for a station, it seems ironical that a number of fires and hurricanes removed several of the early wooden structures. One such disaster was on 29 September 1899 when it is believed that the fire was caused by an overcoat being dried near a stove.

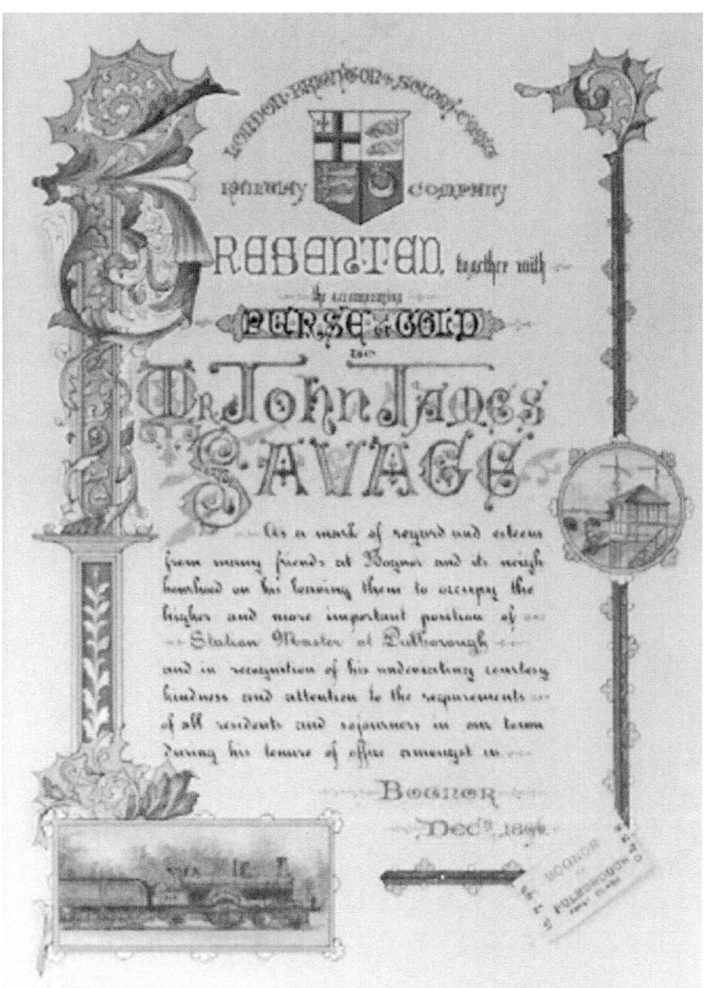

This illuminated scroll was presented to John James Savage when he was transferred to Pulborough Station in December 1896. It was to show the esteem in which he was regarded during his stay at Bognor.

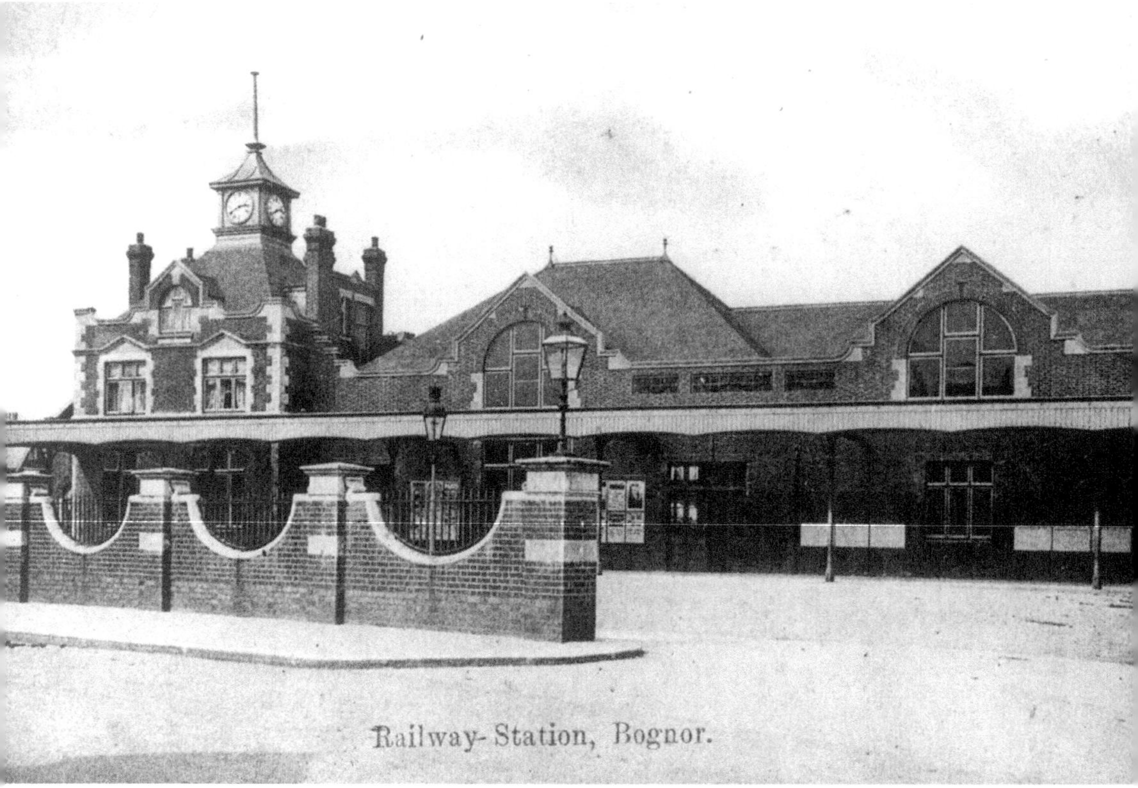
Railway- Station, Bognor.

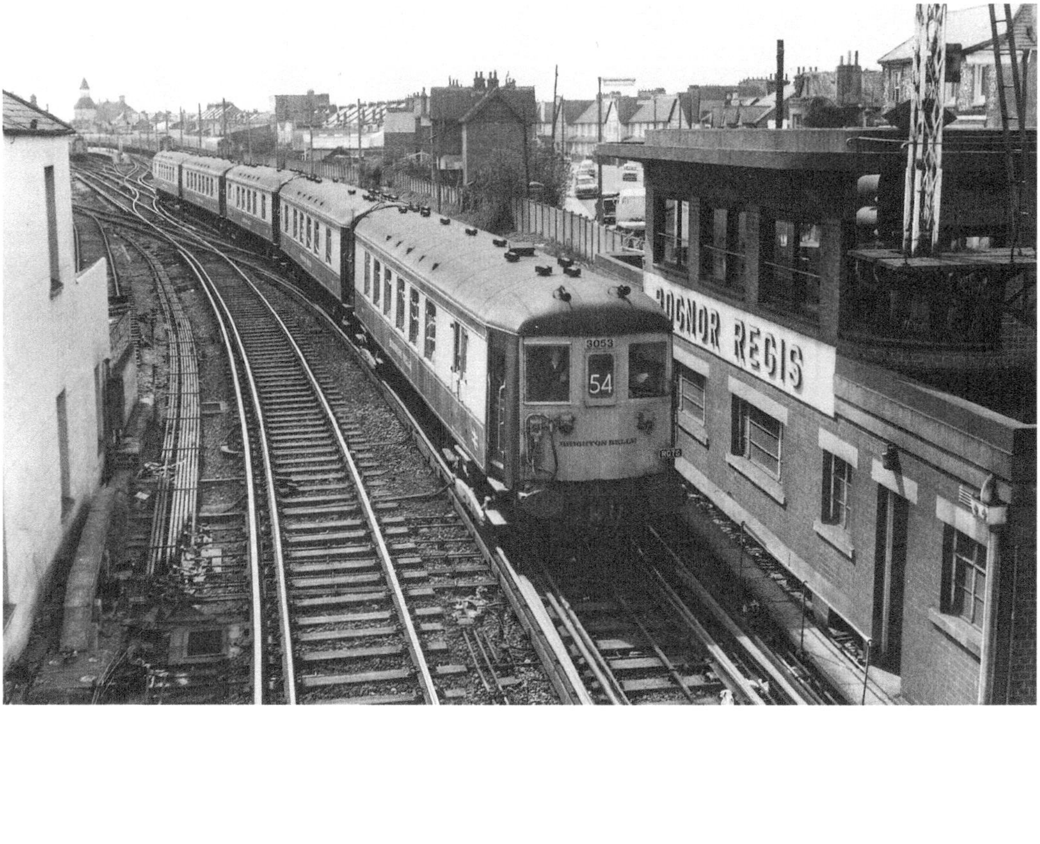
BOGNOR REGIS
3053
54

Advertising was important to encourage visitors, as seen here from a poster used in London. However by 1907 a large number of groups were arriving in the town such as National Sunday League (800) and St Peter's Presbyterian Sunday School (900). In a one week period, nearly 6,000 day trippers arrived in the town. Because of these high figures in 1911 the number of railway lines was doubled to accommodate this increasing trade.

Opposite above: In 1902 the new brick-built railway station was constructed. The company operating at that time was the LBSCR (London Brighton South Coast Railway) and many mementoes of this company can still be found within the fabric of the station.

Opposite below: The original Bersted crossing and signal box were installed in 1876 and replaced in 1938 when the line was electrified. It contained sixty-six levers. This picture is a 1970s view of the signal box.

By the 1920s motor charabancs had replaced the horse-drawn charas. This made excursions easier and quicker and trips to local places of interest more accessible. Many tours operated daily from Bognor and included trips to Slindon, Arundel and Chichester. This particular trip was leaving from the White Horse in Chichester Road to travel to Goodwood Races.

On 2 June 1915 the Southdown Bus Company was formed with the amalgamation of three Sussex concerns: Brighton, Hove and Preston United, the Worthing Motor Services and South Coast Haulage Co. The Bognor home for the Southdown Bus Company was for many years Beach House. The aim of Southdown was that their buses would offer an above average standard of comfort, and would be kept sparkling clean. This is a 1950s advertisement.

The Wesleyan chapel and Sunday school were situated on the north side of the High Street. These buildings were used as garage premises from the 1920s. Bognor Motors put a canopy over the forecourt which hid these two buildings. In 1980 when being demolished to build new shops, these two buildings were briefly seen again.

Arthur Davies was a pioneer in early transport. He is recorded as having the first bus service in the town; he operated from Beach House on the Esplanade from 1903 as 'Motor & Cycle Hire' expanding later to premises in West Street. He operated five charabancs locally as the 'Lady Cars', but due to ill health he sold his business in 1915 to the newly formed Southdown Bus Company.

In their heyday, paddle steamers were a very popular way to explore the coastline. The original landing stage was built in 1901 and was extended in 1936. Numerous postcards have been produced both locally and nationally to show different aspects of the pier. This particular card was produced by R. Briant Burgess who was situated in Waterloo Square.

No seaside resort should be without a trip on the sea. In Bognor Regis, Ron Whittington provided this service alongside his land trains on the seafront. His daughter and grandsons still operate kiosks and the land trains continuing Ron's businesses. Here we can see, from left to right: Dorothy Whittington, Shirley Whittington, Jack Pretlove and Mrs Young.

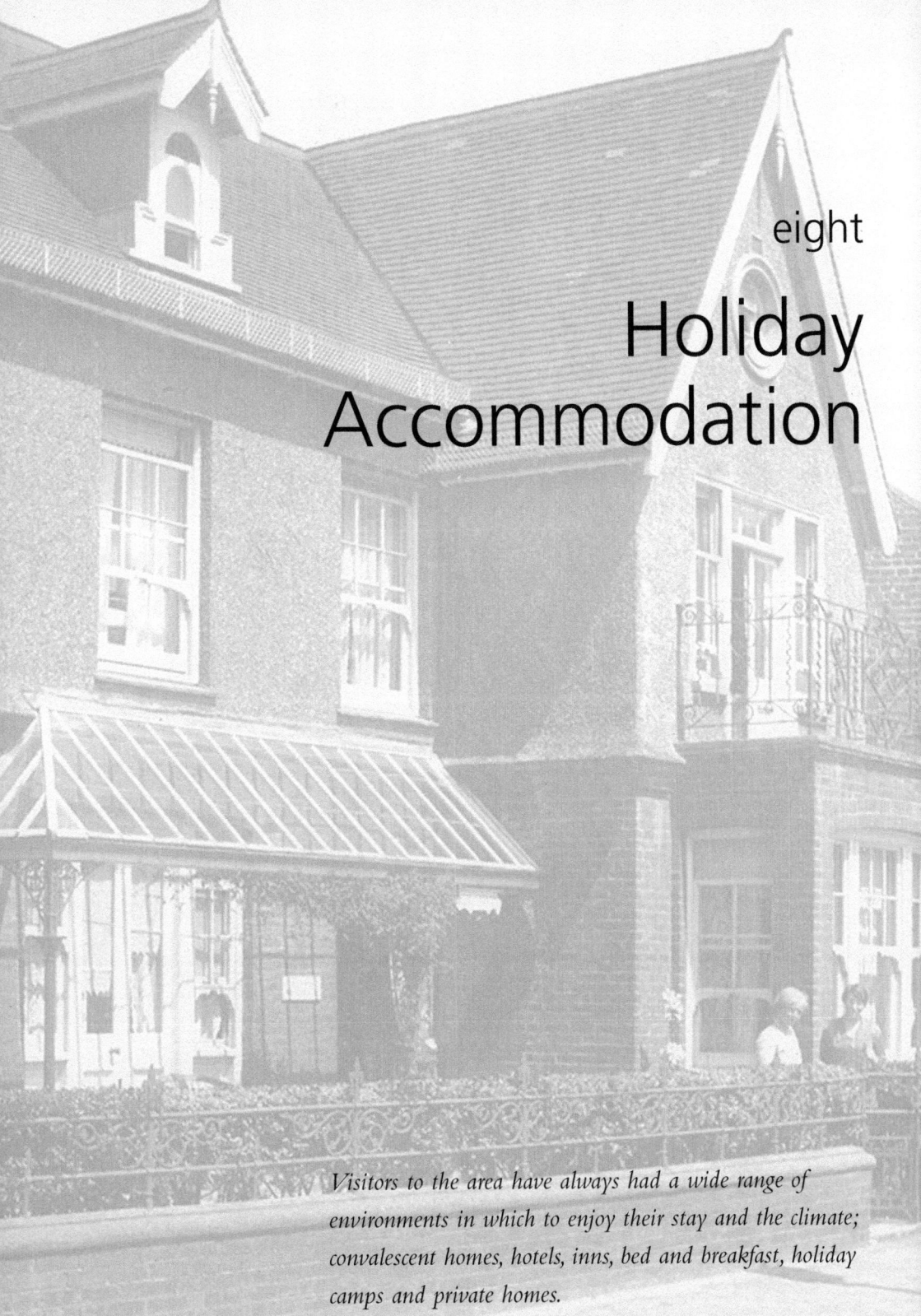

eight

Holiday Accommodation

Visitors to the area have always had a wide range of environments in which to enjoy their stay and the climate; convalescent homes, hotels, inns, bed and breakfast, holiday camps and private homes.

The Royal Norfolk, built in 1830 by Andrew Sorrell, had a balcony added in the 1880s. Three new sections were later added providing the fine present day elevation. Distinguished guests have stayed at the hotel including the exiled Emperor Napoleon III, Queen Alexandra and her sister, the Empress Maude of Russia. Today it is jointly a premier hotel owned by the Revd K. Swadling and the Christ for the Nations UK Bible Training Centre.

The Royal Hotel on the Esplanade overlooks the pier and was built by Richard Dally as a manor house in around 1822 and later leased to Arthur Binstead who opened it as Binstead's Library. Arthur Smith redesigned the house with its impressive frontage and opened it in 1888 as the Royal Pier Hotel. The name was changed to the Royal Hotel in 1912 and in 1960 the windowed lounge extension was added to the left of the building.

The Pyrenees Hotel, which overlooked Marine Park Gardens, was constructed on part of the 23.5-acre site purchased by the Bognor Urban District Council for the Marine Park Gardens Development. The Hotel was ultimately demolished in 1966 and replaced by fifty-six flats.

This building was built in three sections with one section becoming known as the Beaulieu and another the Beaulieu Downs Hotel which was let to Eric St John Foti in 1959 when it was transformed into the Shoreline Club and the Caribbean Hotels. It was used by teenagers for a number of years. Davie Bowie, Reg Dwight (later known as Elton John) and many others played here in June 1966. It was closed in 1968.

The Bridport Hotel was originally opened in 1902 and has now been transformed into separate buildings and apartments. However, Stocker Road was once the site of the Bognor Races and was owned by Dr Stocker. The races operated from the 1840s to 1850s and were well attended events in an area of the town that was ready for development. By 2005 this hotel had been changed into flats.

The earliest record of the Victoria Hotel was 1870; it is believed to have been constructed by Arthur Smith, a local architect and estate agent who was involved in the development of the area. It was mentioned in a H.G. Wells novel, *The Wheels of Chance*, in which it was called the Vicuna Hotel. On this site, there is now a block of flats named Victory Court.

Built by William Hardwicke around 1810 as a coaching inn named the New Inn. In the early days it was just one of the many departure points for the London bound stage coaches. With the growth of the town it became known as the Sussex from the 1840s. Then in 1987 it was renamed the William Hardwicke.

The Russell Hotel was built in 1934 and was a scaled down version of plans announced in 1929 for a hydro-type hotel. In 1967 it was purchased by the London Association for the Blind as a holiday hotel for blind and partially sighted visitors. It was officially opened by Princess Alexandra on 5 July 1968. A new building opened in August 2002 with twenty-first-century facilities.

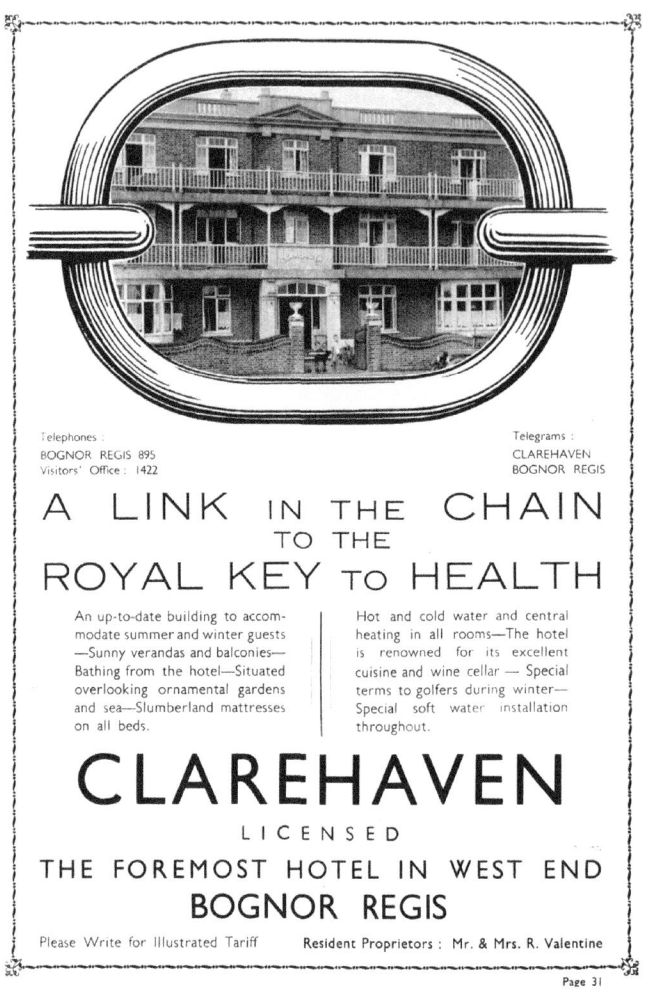

This advertisement from a 1959 holiday brochure depicts a bygone age. The Clarehaven Hotel was situated in Wessex Avenue and whilst it appears to be off the beaten track it is actually only 100 yards from the beach. This interesting building was eventually transformed into flats in 1987/88 which was at a time when many hotels were considered to be underused and thus changed into flats.

Opposite above: The Connaught Hotel situated on the Esplanade. Their 1950s holiday brochure advertised a very comprehensive list of attractions, with all the following available: bathing, two bandstands, bowls, four cinemas, three theatres, three resident concert parties, dancing, tennis and also boating in the form of rowing, sailing, speed and motor boats.

Opposite below: Mr Wonham built eleven houses around 1804 and by the 1850s, they had been joined to form a desirable crescent ready for renting during the summer season. The complete area became empty and lay derelict until 1971. It was partly demolished in 1973 and the remainder cleared in 1982. The area was redeveloped into a complex of forty flats known as the Rock Gardens in 1985.

THE CONNAUGHT HOTEL

The Lounge

The Connaught Hotel is closer to the sea than any other hotel in Bognor Regis. Unrestricted bathing is permitted from the house

Bognor had a large number of convalescent homes, many provided by companies or organisations who wished for their patients to enjoy the benefits of the sea air. Many homes nursed people who came from London, where living conditions were not conducive to good health. This particular home was in Victoria Drive, for staff from the stationers WH Smith Ltd.

Opposite above: Situated in Crescent Road, The Gables is where the early members of Felpham Methodist church met. Living at The Gables in Bognor in 1909, Alice Boyland remarked, 'out east Felpham is growing and there is nothing for folk out there'. She was then to commence a small Sunday school for local boys and girls at No. 1 Sea Road, Felpham.

Opposite below: The 1934 *Guide Book* advertised the Arlington Private Hotel in Norfolk Square, as 'one of the brightest hotels in Bognor'. In 1959 it cost 6-9 guineas per week. All bedrooms had deeply sprung mattresses, electric bed lights and fires. It was ultimately demolished in the 1960s for road widening that never occurred and today is the site of a doctors' surgery.

Originally known as Arthur's Home, this residence was constructed as a home for 'cripples'. It was opened on 16 July 1892 and was a holiday home for fifty children from London in connection with the London Ragged School Union formed by Lord Ashley. It was taken over in 1957 by the Shaftesbury Society and became known as Ashley House. In the twenty-first century it enables young men to enjoy their independence.

Opposite above: Many postcards of this nature would be sent home with a message of 'we are improving and enjoying the seaside'. This would help to advertise the area and various convalescent premises for potential visitors. This card shows Merton Lea, Sylvan Way but changed to St Mary's Holiday Home.

Opposite below: This sketch (*c.*1900) depicts the Mansions but they are also referred to as Victoria Park Terrace, part of the Victoria Park Estate designed and built by Arthur Smith in the 1880s. He was engaged in one of the schemes to develop the town towards the west.

Steyne Cottage at the seaward end of the Steyne was a private residence when it was built in 1819. The central open area of the Steyne was also being developed as private gardens for the Steyne residents. It has been used as a café, restaurant, and public house and in 2006 is Medici's bar and restaurant. The image for this postcard was photographed by Donald Massey, a famous local photographer.

The Faulkner family in 1904, relaxing on the balcony of Gordon House in the Steyne during their stay in Bognor. In those days it was quite usual for families to rent a seaside property for the full summer season.

nine
The Villages

North Bersted, South Bersted, Pagham
Nyetimber, Rose Green, Aldwick, Felpham
Middleton-on-Sea, Elmer

The church of the Holy Cross, originally a small 'cottage church' with a thatched roof. Bishop Durnford of Chichester dedicated this church on 21 June 1880. This early church was replaced in 1894 with a flint and stone building, complete with a small bell tower of cedar wood but without a chancel. In 1939 a temporary chancel and sanctuary were added and these remained until 1969, being replaced in 1972. The distinctive spire was removed in 1976.

Opposite above: It is believed that there had been a building on this site since Elizabethan times. It is a listed building and still retains much of its historic appeal since the first recorded publican in 1842. It is understood that at one time Sir Richard Hotham, Bognor's founder, owned the Royal Oak.

Opposite below: Richard Sharpe of the Rising Sun public house was involved with the Bersted Brass Band. It is reported that the rates paid for a performance by one of the early bands was £5 for a total of eight-and-a-half hours over the Whitsun bank holiday. One of the reasons for forming local Bands prior to the First World War was apparently to 'control the unruly youth'.

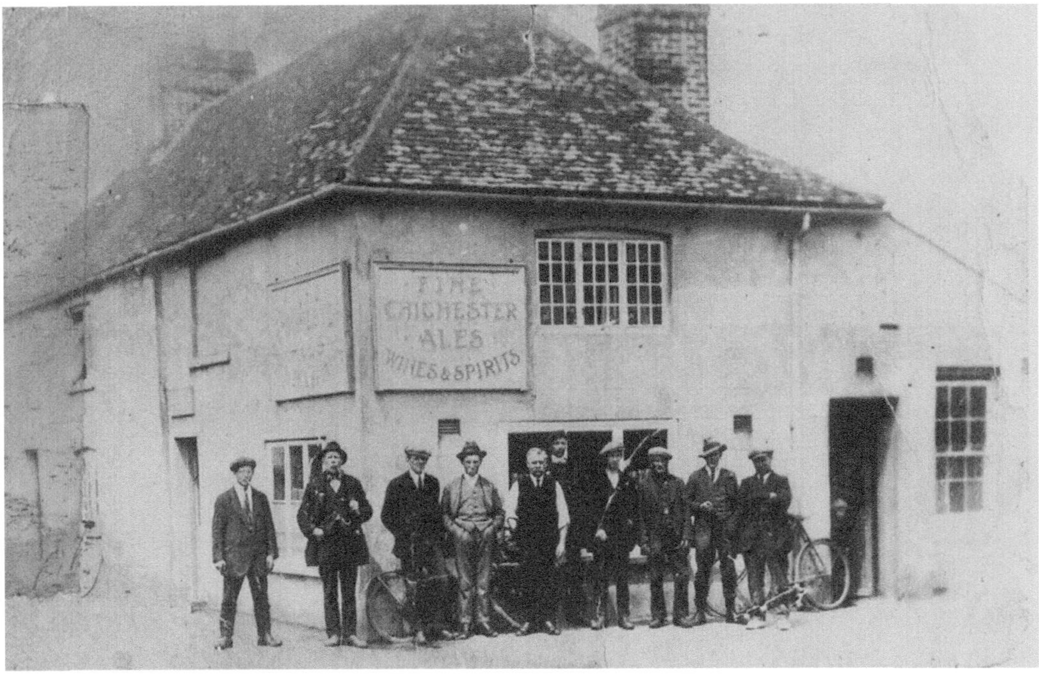
FINE
CHICHESTER
ALES
WINES & SPIRITS

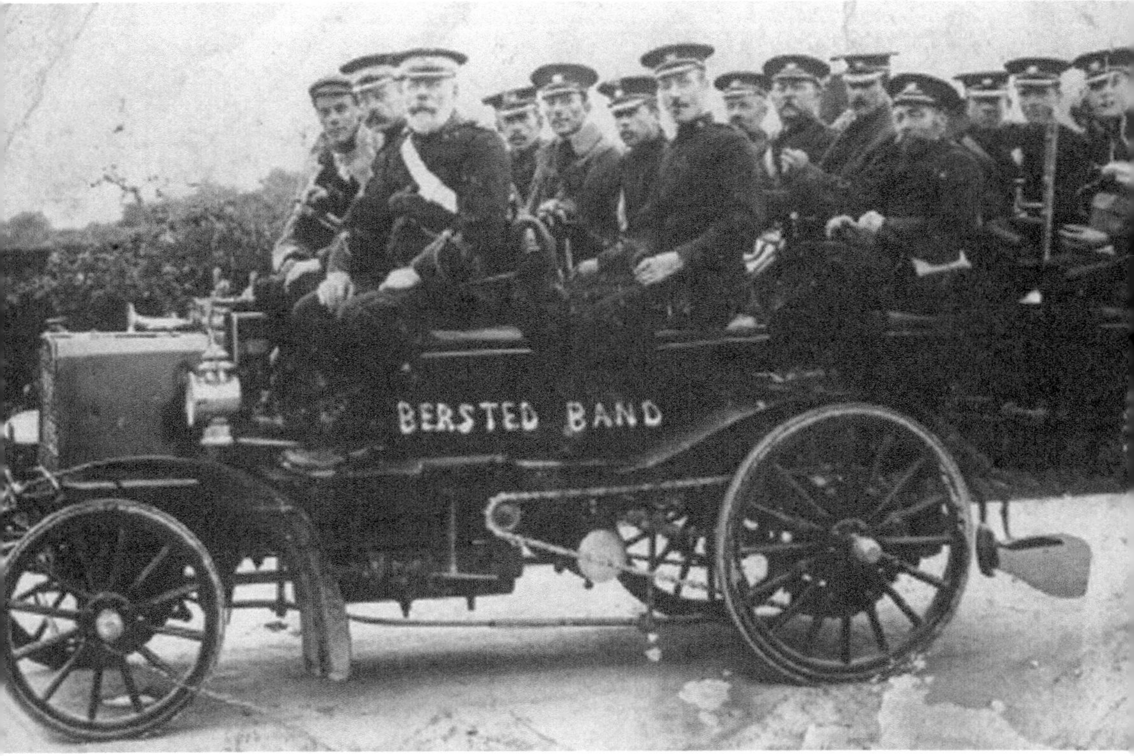
BERSTED BAND

This shop in North Bersted on the corner of Chalcraft Lane and Chichester Road, opposite the Royal Oak has provided a much-needed service for many years. In 2006 it has been replaced with new premises on the ground floor and a number of flats above.

The general stores in South Bersted in 1953 can be clearly seen behind this Ford motor car. Small shops of this nature were prolific in all towns and villages and provided much needed provisions to the community.

This 1906 postcard of the North and South Bersted Cricket Club includes: R. Davies, A. Aylewood, P.C. Dubbin, D. Payne and N. Payne. Both these pictures were produced locally as postcards.

Children from the parish of North Bersted outside the church hall, *c.* 1933. The hall was situated in Chichester Road adjacent to the Holy Cross church. It formed an integral part of the community and was used by all the various groups, clubs etc.

Above: A 1960s view of Chichester Road at its junction with Hawthorn Road. This apparently unhurried scene has been replaced by a busy road junction. However, the shops are still there but with offices and take-away instead of the newsagent and general store.

Left: Mary Wheatland is buried in South Bersted churchyard. She was carried to her final resting place by fishermen from the town's seafront. Her memory lives on in the school children of the town who learn about Mary in their history lessons and who tell their own tales of what it must have been like to live between 1835 and 1924 and in particular, during her time as bathing lady on the seafront.

Opposite above: In 1807, Pagham was described as being 'at least four miles distant from Bognor, and though not much frequented by company, its proximity to the sea, its harbour and situation at the base of a peninsula, claim our notice, or, at least, amply repay the trouble of a visit'. This 1930s postcard view was used to entice a new style of visitor to the area.

The sales particulars of Aldwick Place in 1930 remarked that it was situated in a 'premier residential position with direct frontage to the beach immediately west of Bognor'. It also stated that Aldwick was a favoured coastal village immediately west of Bognor Regis on a delightful stretch of the Sussex coast surrounded by beautiful countryside.

Railway carriages were surplus to the requirements of many railway companies after the First World War and were brought in by road to increase the number of holiday homes but produced a 'shanty town' as seen by residents at the time. Many still remain within a modern construction and occasionally, when a building is being demolished, it is possible to see the original framework of a carriage.

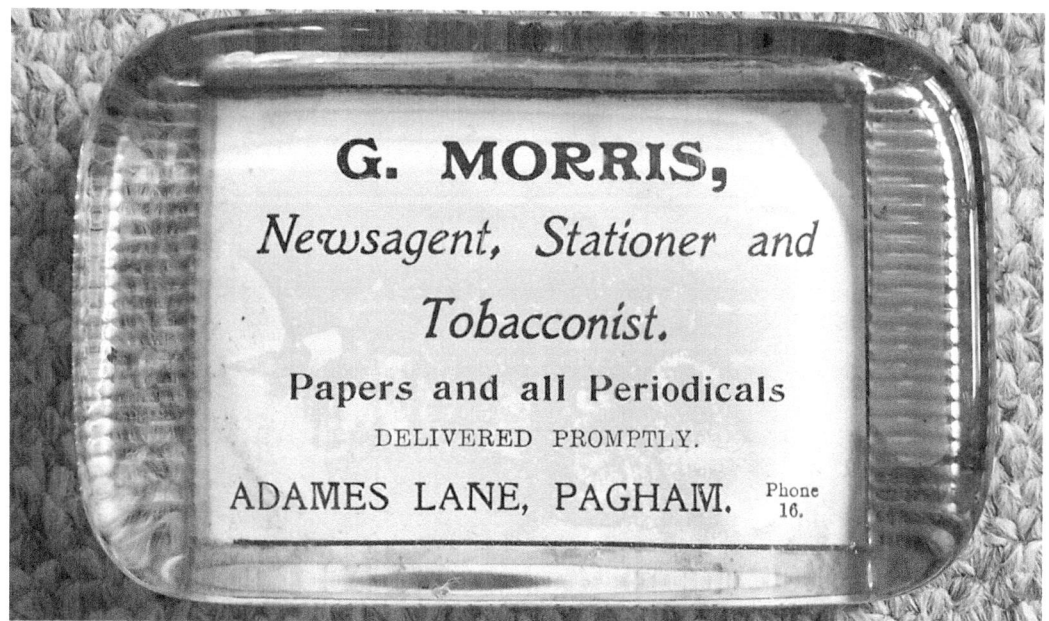

G. Morris was a purveyor of all items for the holiday trade including a range of postcards showing named railway carriages. His address of Adames Lane has been changed to Sea Lane, Pagham, which causes confusion to local and family historians tracing a location.

In 1807 Pagham was recorded as 'a place that affords no bathing, but if you are induced to spend a few weeks and possess sufficient strength and courage, you could commit yourselves to the arms of Neptune, unperceived, and with no less safety and delight than at Bognor'. By 1907 the first caravan had arrived for a Miss Carre who paid £1 10s per year. The growth of caravans resulted in the Church Farm Holiday centre.

The Riviera Lido Holiday Club opened in 1938 and closed in 1985 after providing a seaside retreat for many people. In the early days these styles of holidays were to provide healthy outdoor sports. During the Second World War it was used by the Ministry of Health for 'physically defective children' and then as a barracks for the RAF. In 1987 the area was transformed into a housing complex.

Above: The original alehouse in Pagham was owned by the Turner family in 1840 and used by smugglers. In 1930 the original premises were demolished and replaced by today's larger building. It is just one of the pubs visited on the annual Boxing Day pram race which started in 1946 and raises money for local charities and organisations.

Above: The Thatched Cottage in Fish Lane, Aldwick has been occupied for over 300 years by the same family. This reminder of yesteryear is today the home of a twenty-first-century website designer.

Right: This family photograph, taken prior to 1904, is outside the thatched cottage in Fish Lane, Aldwick and includes, standing in the back row from left to right: James Williams, Annie Ada (James' wife) and Charles Brown. Seated in the front row are: Theophilus Williams, Maria Roselle (sister of Annie), Fanny Williams (Christmas) mother of the two boys and finally Elizabeth Christmas. Unfortunately we were not able to name the children.

Opposite below: This delightful 1930s postcard shows a corner of St Thomas A'Becket church. It is typical of the era when postcards were produced to cover a wide range of unusual subjects. Most churches had postcard views printed depicting internal, external and even the graveyard views.

Above: Following the visit of King George V in 1929, Craigweil House was eventually demolished to make way for housing within a private estate here named as Craigweil-on-Sea. Visitors to the town still request the location of Craigweil House.

Opposite below: Holiday makers have always taken photographs to remind them of their visit to the seaside. Here a family group is situated near the Tamarisk Hedge, Aldwick. The dress code for this relaxing holiday is a long way from the dress code of the twenty-first century.

Right: The Black Tower Mill in Nyetimber was built around 1840. With the advent of the First World War and damaged machinery the life of the mill came to an end. The base continued to be used as a carpenter's shop, but in 1927 the sweeps were damaged by lightning. Following a fire in June 1962, the Revd John Maynard dug the first spit in 1981 for the foundation of retirement homes, here depicted by Martin Venables.

Below: In the vicinity of Pagham and Aldwick, housing grew as the need for homes increased. Many of these areas had their own residents' associations and these associations were seen as the forerunners of the Parish Councils. Rose Green, rarely depicted on postcards, shows off its busy shopping centre.

Nyetimber Mill,

One of the earliest records of the Black Mill is of William Cosens in 1801 purchasing an area named Mill Field for the sum of £555. In the 1880s the mill had ceased to be active and by the 1890s had lost its sails. It was finally demolished in 1907. The area in this vicinity, which ran down to the sea, had become known as the Felpham Mill Building Estate.

In 1907 Ameys, a Petersfield brewer, took over the Black Mill site and built a general store and off-license, using bricks from the demolished mill as foundation material. Henry Snook eventually took this over in 1916. As late as 1966 the buildings were still called 'The Old Mill Off-License' and the advertising board outside showed a windmill. Today this corner of the village is always referred to as 'Snook's Corner'.

A young Reg Came on holiday in 1935 with Mr and Mrs Williams and their daughter, enjoying the sunshine on the balcony of their railway carriage holiday home in Felpham. This part of the coast was seen very much as a superior holiday destination. These railway carriages were in Sea Road, a very popular holiday choice for many years.

Mrs Florence Densley with Mr Pearce in the 1930s outside their shop, the Felpham Stores. Florence ran it on her own for ten years until 1957 when her son Eric and his wife Barbara took over and continued for the next twenty-one years. In total Florence and Eric ran the Felpham Stores for fifty-six years. It was, until the middle of 2006, a fish and chip shop and restaurant.

Above: Turret House was built in 1797 by William Hayley, a popular poet and patron of the arts. In 1800, Hayley commissioned William Blake to carry out sculpture work within the library. The building had a number of occupants including the Fire Service, who used it after 1942. In the 1950s it was occupied briefly by a theological college who also advertised their Biblical Museum. It was demolished in 1961 and replaced by flats.

Left: The Parish church of St Mary the Virgin has sections dating from around 1100. The Lych Gate was erected in 1897 to commemorate Queen Victoria's Diamond Jubilee. A stone on the outer wall records: 'To the glory of God and in commemoration of Queen Victoria's Diamond Jubilee'. It also notes that F.H. Talbot was the vicar, GES, Streatfield the architect and T. Start the builder. It forms an impressive entrance to the church.

Right: This sketch shows the Brewers Arms which is alleged to have been an alehouse from the eighteenth century. It was eventually closed and demolished when the current Southdowns Hotel was built in 1924.

Below: The laying of the foundation stone of the Felpham Methodist church by Alice Boyland on 7 June 1939. The premises at that time consisted of a church hall, schoolroom, vestry and kitchen. Miss Boyland had worked tirelessly to establish a church in Felpham and was to see it materialise with this ceremony.

Above: The shops in Middleton-on-Sea are near the site of the 1920s Coldicott homes. Captain H. Rowland Coldicott was the person to whom much of the development of this area is attributed. His idea was to create a residential area and a village community, complete with its own facilities. Upon the retirement of Captain Coldicott in 1937 the Middleton-on-Sea Association was formed to continue with his vision of the village environment.

This postcard view of Pixies' Lodge was obviously produced for the holiday trade to enable visitors to send home with the message, 'this is where we are staying'. It is a typical Coldicott semi-detached which was built in the 1920s by Middleton builders.

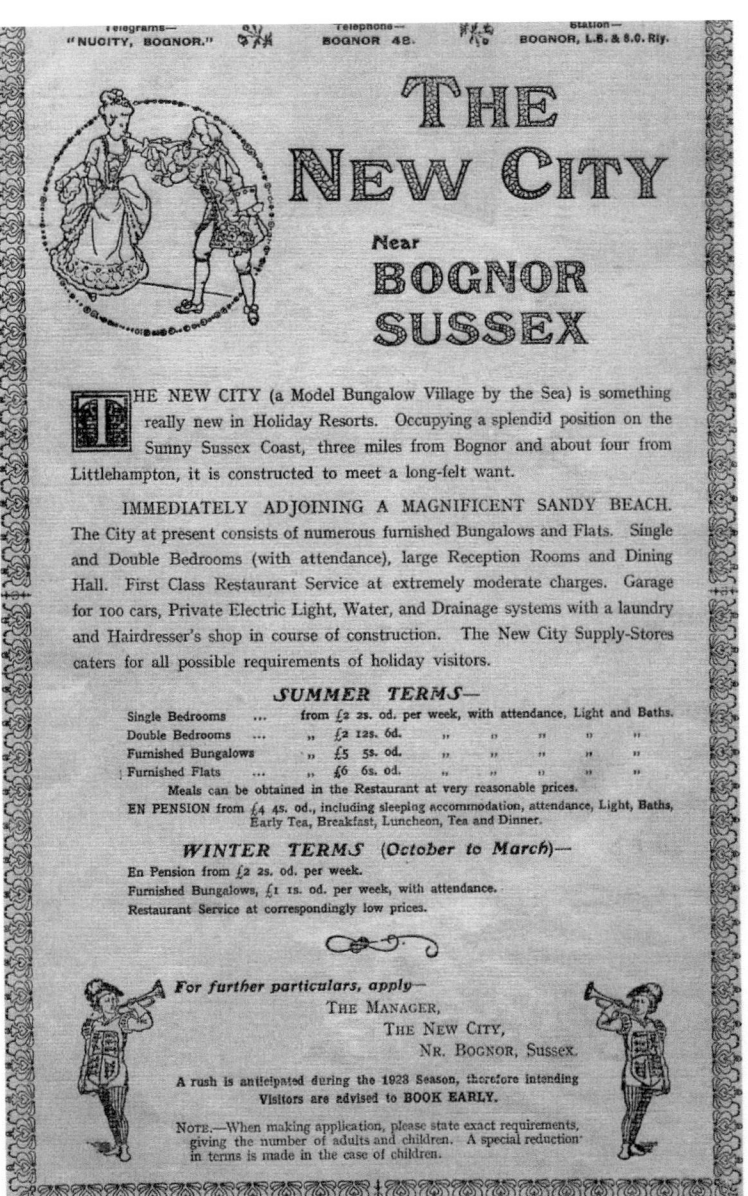

Middleton was still sufficiently unknown at this time that the suffix of Bognor was necessary on this advertisement to advise all those new holiday makers of the locality of their holiday home.

The Norman Thompson Flight Co. Ltd produced sea planes during the First World War in Middleton-on-Sea and employed people from the surrounding area. On closing one of the hangars became the Pavilion Entertainment Centre in Bognor. The site has now disappeared beneath housing.

Middleton and Elmer were very popular destinations and the opportunity arose for the construction of the New City Bognor by 1923. This was a 'holiday centre' of the period.

This 1940s postcard view of the Elmer Hotel would seem to be almost the same view as seen in the 1930s when it was constructed. The Elmer Hotel in 2006 boasts the same uncluttered view but with a change of menu and façade for the residents and annual visitors to the area.

Betty & Wilfred Richards with Ann aged two on the beach at Middleton-on-Sea during the summer of 1939, looking towards Old Point. Bognor Regis and the villages were, and continue to be, an attraction on the South Coast of Great Britain.

Other local titles published by The History Press

Littlehampton Revisited
ROLF ZEEGERS, JULIET NYE AND LUCY ASHBY

Illustrated with over 200 captivating photographs, *Littlehampton Revisited* takes the reader on a fascinating journey through this seaside resort. Rolf Zeegers brings to life times old and new through the eyes of the people who lived and worked in the town. The book will also bring back nostalgic memories to all those who spent happy holidays here.

978 07524 3987 7

Horsham Streets
SYLVIA BARLOW

A thriving and bustling market town, Horsham is a place with a sense of its own identity. From its early origins it is well known for its sheep, cattle and corn markets with charters for the markets having been granted by the King from the thirteenth century. Illustrated with over 100 evocative photographs and ephemera, this absorbing book captures Horsham's heritage and offers a unique glimpse into the town's past.

978 0 7524 4305 8

Haunted Brighton
ALAN MURDIE

From heart-stopping accounts of apparitions, manifestations and related supernatural phenomena to first-hand encounters with polite ghosts, malign presences and poltergeists, this collection of stories contains both well-known and hitherto unpublished cases of hauntings from in and around Brighton. This book is bound to captivate anyone interested in the supernatural history of the area.

978 07524 3829 0

Portsmouth at War
ANDREW WHITMARSH

Portsmouth at War is a pictorial record of the events of the Second World War as they impacted on the people of the city. Illustrated with over 200 original photographs, many sourced from The News' extensive archives, this book provides a unique insight into wartime life, recreating vividly the tragedy, heroism, austerity and humour of these years. Researched by the curator of the Portsmouth's D-Day Museum, this work will stir powerful memories for any resident of the city during this turbulent time.

978 07524 4296 9

If you are interested in purchasing other books published by The History Press, or in case you have difficulty finding any of our books in your local bookshop, you can also place orders directly through our website
www.thehistorypress.co.uk